# Reclaim Your Relationship

*A Workbook of Exercises and Techniques to Help You Reconnect with Your Partner*

Ronald T. Potter-Efron, M.S.W., Ph.D.

Patricia S. Potter-Efron, M.S.

WILEY

John Wiley & Sons, Inc.

*We dedicate this workbook to our children, their spouses, and their children: Jenny, Jeff, and Elizabeth Berger, Josh Potter-Efron, and Cindy, Mark, David, and Christopher Keith*

The book is printed on acid-free paper. ∞

Copyright © 2006 by Ronald T. Potter-Efron and Patricia S. Potter-Efron. All rights reserved

Published by John Wiley & Sons, Inc., Hoboken, New Jersey
Published simultaneously in Canada

Design and composition by Navta Associates, Inc.

For general information about our other products and services, please contact our Customer Care Department within the United States at (800) 762-2974, outside the United States at (317) 572-3993 or fax (317) 572-4002.

Wiley also publishes its books in a variety of electronic formats. Some content that appears in print may not be available in electronic books. For more information about Wiley products, visit our web site at www.wiley.com.

ISBN-10 0-471-74932-X
ISBN-13 978-0-471-74932-5

Printed in the United States of America

10  9  8  7  6  5  4  3  2  1

# Contents

# Acknowledgments

We want to thank several people for their help. Eileen Immerman initially prepared this book for publication, doing her usual fine job. Working with Eileen is a pleasure.

Amy Walker reviewed most of the exercises, giving us wonderful feedback. She and her husband, Aaron, have also inspired us with their loving relationship.

Many of our clients at First Things First Counseling tried out selected exercises. We can't name these people because of confidentiality, but we are grateful. Their responses led to useful and sometimes drastic revisions of the exercises.

The people at First Things First Counseling, both professional colleagues and office staff, have talked with us about the book and shared their own perspectives. Thanks go to Shawn Allen, Kathy Anderson, Richard Fuhrer, Linda Klitzke, Dar Olson, Bruce Pamperin, Jennifer Parker, Carla Peterson, Ed Ramsey, Dr. Bhashkar Reddy, Dave Stratton, and Susan Turell.

Stacey Glick, our agent at Dystelt Goderich Literacy Management, was remarkably persistent in seeking and eventually finding the best home for this workbook.

Finally, we thank our editors at John Wiley, including Teryn Johnson, Kimberly Monroe-Hill, and Sibylle Kazeroid, for turning our initial project into a completed product.

# Introduction

"I love you."

Why is this single phrase so important?

Sure, it's always nice to hear it. But why does it seem like life is incomplete unless you can say "I love you" to others and hear them saying it to you? The answer, of course, is that people are programmed for love. The bonding that occurs between mother and baby sets the stage for all future significant relationships. Without that immediate, hardwired connection between parent and infant, children simply would not survive. The core meaning of "I love you" for a parent is "You are so important to me that I will do everything in my power to ensure your survival." This commitment doesn't feel like a sacrifice, however. It is a promise made from deep within the parent's soul. Meanwhile, the infant absorbs and returns the parent's love since he or she is also hardwired to bond. The child's message to the parent is "I love you, too. I will accept your caring and feel close to you."

Loved infants usually grow up to become adults capable of sharing this sense of special closeness with others. Indeed, love feels so wonderful that they search for people to whom they can say "I love you." Parental substitutes. Friends. Most of all, partners with whom they can make love, share secrets, raise a family, and feel connected. It's then that "I love you" begins to take on multiple meanings, such as:

You are special.

You give meaning to my life.

I think of you often.

I want to make you happy.

You are a wonderful friend.

I can talk to you about anything.

I have a feeling of warmth, closeness, and familiarity with you.

I would grieve if I lost you.

## What Keeps People from Saying "I Love You"?

Since "I love you" is such a clear sentence, you'd think it would be very easy to say. "I love you." "I love you." "I love you." There. That wasn't difficult. Indeed, there would be little need for a workbook on this topic if everybody could just let those words roll out whenever they wished. But life is not that simple. In fact, many people have trouble expressing their love. Let us briefly describe the three most common problems we've noticed.

1. *Some people can't say "I love you."* The words seem to get stuck in their throats. They may very well feel love for their partner, children, parents, and friends, but they just cannot convince themselves to say so. These people may work all day to support their families but then fail to tell them how much they matter. They sometimes hope that others will know they love them without their having to say it out loud. They believe that their supportive actions should be enough to show others that they love them. "After all," they might say, "that's why I work so hard and do so much for them."

2. *Some people can't show their love.* These people have the opposite problem from the group above. They can tell and do tell others they love them. Unfortunately, their actions don't match their words. Most of these people aren't mean-spirited, greedy, or self-centered. They are simply neglectful of others, failing to do the many small things in life

that show their partner that he or she is treasured. *We need both to tell our partners and to show them that we love them.* And certainly *we need our partners both to tell us and to show us we are loved.* Neither saying "I love you" nor doing loving things is enough by itself.

3. *Some people can't take in their partner's love.* Nothing is more frustrating than telling someone how much you love him or her only to have your words brushed off with an "uh-huh; that's nice" as if they are simply crumbs. While some of these people neither give nor receive love, many of them are really quite loving. It's just that they feel far more comfortable giving love to others than taking it in.

   *It's just as important, in the long run, to take in your partner's love as it is to express yours.* A relationship isn't complete until each partner can both give and receive love.

## Key Concepts and Beliefs That Form the Basis of This Book

- We define *love* as "a profoundly tender, passionate affection for another person" (*Random House Unabridged Dictionary*, Second Edition).*

- We believe that love can be expressed to one's partner in many ways, with both words and deeds. Most people will feel more loved if their partner demonstrates love in more than one or two ways.

- We think that people can continually develop new ways to show love to their partner. Finding ways to tell one's partner "I love you" is a continuing opportunity for creativity.

- We believe that saying "I love you" (and meaning it) is one of the greatest ways for any human being to connect with another and prevent the feelings of loneliness and isolation we might otherwise endure.

---

*We are primarily concerned in this workbook with the love between two adult partners. This "romantic love" usually includes sexuality, commitment, friendship, and a feeling that there is a special bond between the partners.

- We suggest that receiving (and accepting) the gift of another's love helps most people feel deeply honored, appreciated, and attached. Certainly for many people, the single best present they can give is to help their partner feel loved. But receiving another's love is also a great gift.

   On the other hand, none of us owes anyone else a single "I love you." This phrase should always be given voluntarily—a gift that comes with no strings attached. That is one reason being loved feels so wonderful; it is one individual's offering of deep connection that can never be earned, owed, or demanded.

- We know that no one word can ever express all the aspects of love. That's why *love* has so many synonyms, such as *tenderness, fondness, warmth, passion, devotion, cherish,* and *adore.* We will help you increase your love vocabulary so you can find the right words at the right time to say "I love you" in exactly the best way.

- We feel that the phrase "I love you" is an offer of mutual connection. It works best, then, when the message is clearly stated by one person and clearly responded to by another. That's why "Well, he should have known I loved him when I [said . . . or did . . .]" ways of demonstrating love can be so frustrating. No one should have to play a guessing game to figure out whether he or she is loved.

- We admit that telling another person you love him or her always carries the risk of rejection, as in "Well, I don't love you" or "Uh-huh" or "Do you always have to say that?" But that's what makes saying those words so special. Sure, telling someone you love him or her gives that person the opportunity to hurt you. However, expressing love is so important, the risk is often worth taking. You're telling your partner you have a wonderful gift to offer if he or she wants it—the gift of an enduring, soulful embrace.

- We understand that allowing love in can feel risky. Feeling the strength of another's love can make you feel exposed and vulnerable. Besides, how can you be sure that the other person means what he or she is saying? Even if he or she does, how can you be sure that he or she won't eventually fall out of love with you, leaving you feeling alone and abandoned? Yet again, for most people this is a risk worth taking simply because human beings have such a deep need to feel loved.

This book is written with a spirit of adventure. Are you willing to risk the unknown by exploring your ability to share the words and feelings of love? If so, you might add depth, richness, wonder, and beauty to the most important relationship in your life.

## The Three Main Sources for This Workbook

We've crafted forty-six exercises for this workbook, largely from three sources. One is academic, one is professional, and one is profoundly personal. The academic source comprises several theories and bodies of research. One of the best of these is the fifty-plus years of thought and research in the area of attachment and bonding begun by John Bowlby and Mary Ainsworth, who studied infants' attachment to their mothers. More recently, this focus on attachment has been transferred into the area of adult bonding by such researchers as Mary Main and Kim Bartholomew. To put matters simply, all these writers document that humans crave deep, intimate connection with other humans. When this need is well met, at first by parents who can offer their children consistent physical safety and emotional nourishment, people emerge feeling quite secure. Secure people at any age feel both loved and loving. Saying "I love you" comes pretty easily to them because they live in a warm and caring world.

However, not all parents can consistently meet their children's security needs. As a result, some children become anxious and cling to their parents, while others find psychological refuge by retreating from the field of love. "If I don't let myself need my parents," they seem to think, "then I won't ever have to feel the pain of their not being there for me when I need them." Later, as adults, the anxious children often develop into "Preoccupied" adults who never feel assured of another's love ("Do you love me? I mean, do you really love me?" they may ask repeatedly). Those who have retreated become "Dismissers," who avoid the whole messy area of love and commitment. Some people even develop both anxious and dismissive behaviors. Kim Bartholomew labels these persons "Fearful" because of their hesitation to enter into relationships even though they badly want to find love. Attachment theory, then, is useful in two ways: it points to what constitutes love in all intimate relationships and it points out specific kinds of problems that can make the expression of love difficult. Most specifically, Dismissive individuals need to learn that saying "I love you" won't leave them incredibly vulnerable and certain to be disappointed. They also have to let other people love them without blowing them off. Preoccupied persons must learn graciously how to take in the love that is offered. Fearful individuals need to learn both of these tasks. Meanwhile, basically Secure individuals must remember to keep practicing the art of loving others and not let that tremendous gift be lost in the busy rushing lives they lead.

Another academic source for our ideas comes from the research and writings of John Gottman. For years Gottman has studied couples in and out of conflict. He has discovered that couples who live relatively happily together, avoiding both divorce and perpetual animosity, aren't just good problem solvers. They do handle conflict well, in large part by accepting each other's differences, but they do two other things as well. First, they take the time and energy to really learn about each other, creating what Gottman calls "love maps." Taking the time and energy to understand your partner helps ensure that each partner gives the other what that person most wants and needs to feel loved. Second, these successful couples are affectionate with each other even during conflict. That means "I love you" is said, or expressed, consistently.

The second source for this book is our twenty-some years as professional marriage therapists. Frankly, couples counseling is often hard work, made especially poignant by watching two people unnecessarily hurt each other again and again. By the time most couples see us they have forgotten how to say "I love you" to each other. They've also forgotten how to show each other their love. As for taking in the other's love, forget it. These people don't trust each other much anymore, so they are very cautious about accepting each other's offers of kindness, caring, or love.

Still, many couples do get better. After all, they became partners for a reason. At one time they mostly loved, respected, and trusted each other. They come to counseling just wanting to get back on the path of love.

The third source for this book is our forty-year marriage, a union that has endured opposing personalities, alcohol and drug addiction, Pat's heart attack, a short separation, raising three feisty children, and all the usual challenges to mutual commitment spanning a four-decade relationship. We'd like to tell you that we said "I love you" to each other every day, that we showed that love every day, that we took in each other's love every day. But of course that would be untrue. We're human, and we've had our share of times when "I love you" was hardly the first thing we said to each other when we awoke or the last words we spoke at night. But we can say this: even in the worst of times, "I love you" always felt right. "I love you" (spoken and demonstrated and taken in) has helped heal the worst wounds while enriching the good days of our marriage.

## Ten Reasons to Read This Book and Do These Exercises

1.  *You can always improve your skills when it comes to expressing love.*

    Say "I love you." Show your love. Take love in. Think of these three actions as skills that can be continually improved upon when you love someone. You can get better and better at all three, but only with thoughtfulness, effort, and creativity. On the other hand, we tend to lose skills that we don't practice. So even if you are fortunate enough to be in a loving and satisfying relationship right now, the best way to maintain the status quo is to improve your skills in these areas.

2.  *You deserve validation and encouragement for what you are doing well.*

    "Hey, I do that already!" We're pretty sure you'll have that thought at least a few times as you read through these exercises. Good. Then keep doing those things that help bring love into your relationship. Give yourself credit for being able to give and receive this wonderful mutual gift.

3. *You may feel a need to renew your relationship with your partner.*

Perhaps you two are caught up in the rush of raising a family and are beginning to lose contact with each other as a couple. Or maybe your careers have gradually taken priority over your relationship. You've slowly drifted apart, but now you're looking for a way to reconnect. The exercises in this book could help you rediscover your love.

4. *You may be just developing a relationship (or even thinking about beginning one) and want to tune in to the special needs of that new person in your life.*

One of the great secrets in love is to give your partner the gifts he or she really wants, not just what you think or hope will be appreciated. But how can you know what your partner wants? By taking the time to ask, by observing carefully what he or she says and does, and perhaps by sharing the exercises and thoughts in this book.

5. *You may need help learning how to show love because you didn't get much modeling when you were growing up.*

American families run the "I love you" gamut from highly demonstrative ("We said 'I love you' twenty times a day when I was growing up") to completely nondemonstrative ("We never even saw my parents hug, much less say they loved each other"). You may have grown up on the nondemonstrative side, and because of that you simply never learned how to say "I love you." You may be good at showing your love by being a good provider and/or by doing many things for your family, but remember this: *The people you love need both to hear and to see that they are loved.* Showing them you love them is great, but you need to tell them you love them, too. The exercises in this book will help you learn a skill that will greatly enhance your feelings of connection with your loved ones.

6. *You may need to give yourself permission to be more loving and to take in the love of others.*

In his masterly writings on shame, Gershen Kaufman discusses how sometimes children are taught that giving or receiving love is a bad thing to do. The very idea of nurturing or being nurtured then becomes "shame-bound." If that has happened to you, you probably sense that you would be weak, bad, or stupid to give love to others and/or to accept love offerings even from those closest to you. This area is somewhat gender-specific. Chances are that if you are male you have been taught that showing too much love is unmasculine and will turn you into a wimp. Women are often taught the opposite: receiving love and caring is not okay because they should only give and give. So, if you fit that pattern and are male you will benefit especially from the sections on giving love, while females might especially need to focus on receiving love.

7. *You may have developed the habit of mostly looking for what's wrong with your partner instead of what's right, and now you want to change that pattern.*

   Perhaps you were raised by parents who were very critical of you or each other. You learned from them to search for the bad things the people you love do and to call attention to those things instead of noticing and commenting on your loved ones' positive qualities. Or maybe over the years you have slowly become more negative and critical with your partner. However you developed this habit of criticizing, reading this book might help you get better at looking for ways to accept, appreciate, and even admire your partner.

8. *You may just be recovering from a wounding relationship or experiences that have affected your ability to be loving.*

   Sometimes love goes wrong. Perhaps your partner cheated on you. Maybe alcohol or drugs interfered with his or her (or your) ability to take responsibility. Or perhaps you fell away from each other until it was too late to salvage the relationship. Maybe you are recovering from childhood sexual abuse, or you're the survivor of a more recent relationship with someone who was physically or emotionally abusive toward you. The result is that you've lost faith that real love between two people is possible. You have gotten caught up in a world of doubt, distrust, cynicism, and despair—and yet you want to regain your faith in yourself and the world. You want to believe again that you can love and be loved. Taking the time to do these exercises, slowly and even cautiously, may help you reclaim your right to be loved and loving.

9. *You may suffer from the "broken cup" syndrome, never feeling that you get enough love, and now you want to learn better how to accept the love that is offered without always demanding more.*

   If people often tell you how much they love you, but you never feel satisfied, you may be suffering from the "broken cup" syndrome. Your cup never runs over. In fact, it always feels almost empty to you. If this is your situation, you will want to pay particular attention to the third part of this workbook, the section that will help you learn to take in and appreciate the love that is offered to you.

10. *You and your partner may have been going through hard times with each other. You've had too much conflict, too much anger, too much distancing. Now the two of you want to rekindle your love and affection but need a few ideas on how to get started.*

    Few relationships are perpetually pleasant. Realistically, most couples go through periods of discomfort, during which they are less than loving with each other. Indeed, you and your partner may be in the middle or at the end of one such period now. Going through the exercises in this book together is one way for the two of you to reconnect and rekindle your love.

### How to Read This Book

We hope that both you and your partner are reading this book and doing the exercises together. However, we've designed this workbook so that most of the exercises can be done alone. There are portions of some exercises that suggest you talk with your partner or get information from him or her. If you don't happen to have someone in your life right now, you can skip those parts—or you can take the role of a past actual partner or a future hoped-for partner and answer those questions with the help of your imagination.

We recommend that you take your time with these exercises. First, skim through all forty-six exercises (each is preceded by a discussion about why that particular exercise is useful). Then decide which section is most important for you to begin with: telling people you love them, showing them that it's true, or taking in love from others. And then start doing the exercises, at the rate of about one a day, beginning with the one or two that will help you the most right away. You may find that a few of the exercises are worth doing several times over the course of a year—the exercises that mean the most will help you keep walking on a loving path.

If you are doing these exercises with your partner, we suggest you each select one exercise that you think will help *you* the most rather than one that you think your partner most needs to work on. By keeping the focus on yourself, you won't come across as telling your partner what to do but as willing to learn and change to help make the relationship better. But make sure each of you does both exercises, and share the results before selecting another two to work on. Also, commit to making your sharing a positive, loving experience. Remember, the goal here is for each of you to feel more loved, not more criticized, so keep the emphasis on creating a mutually enjoyable experience.

# PART ONE

# How to Say "I Love You"

# Practice, practice, practice: Developing the positive habit of saying "I love you"

The goal of this exercise is to help you develop the positive habit of saying "I love you" to your partner several times every day. It sounds simple enough, doesn't it? After all, "I love you" is a simple declarative sentence consisting of three short words. But people are masters at turning something easy into something difficult. We make life complicated, especially when it comes to relationships. We create inner turmoil by asking questions like "Should I tell her I love her?"; "Will he tell me he loves me if I say it first?"; "I'd like to say 'I love you,' but I don't know how"; and "But don't you have to really *feel* loving to say 'I love you'?"

Forget all that stuff. Saying "I love you" doesn't have to be complicated, confusing, or difficult. You just say it. Then you say it again. And again. The more often you tell your partner that you love him or her, the easier it gets. Eventually, you develop a positive habit. That's when saying "I love you" becomes a constant in your relationship. And only then, when both partners say "I love you" to each other every day, do they feel really safe with each other. There is simply no substitute for hearing those words.

Here is a dos and don'ts list for developing the positive habit of regularly saying "I love you" to your partner.

> **SMART START**
>
> *First, walk the path.*
> —AFRICAN PROVERB

15

## Do

- *Say "I love you" to your partner at least three times a day.*

  When it comes to saying "I love you," quality is important, but there is no substitute for quantity. Keep saying "I love you" until it becomes totally natural and comfortable.

- *Push through any blocks or hesitations you have about saying "I love you."*

  Shyness, stubbornness, fear of rejection, fear of vulnerability, fatigue, anxiety, depression—these emotions are all real and painful. But don't let them stop you from saying the most important thing you can ever say to another person.

- *Say "I love you" even when you are feeling irritated, bothered, annoyed, or upset with your partner.*

  Saying "I love you" in the middle of a disagreement is a wonderful way to lessen tension and reassure both yourself and your partner that no conflict will destroy your love.

- *For a while, keep track of how many times a day you say "I love you."*

  Be a scientist; collect data. At the end of the day, make a note, mental or written, of how many times you said "I love you" to your partner. If it was less than three, ask yourself what went wrong that day so you can make some changes tomorrow.

- *Listen to yourself as you say "I love you" and notice how it feels.*

  Pay attention to how you say "I love you" and how you feel as you say it. Can you hear the caring in your voice? Do your words sound more like a question than a statement? Do you feel relaxed? Comfortable?

- *Sneak in a few "I love you"s in unexpected situations.*

  There is no bad time to say "I love you." Add a little playfulness to your routine by throwing in an "I love you" while making a shopping list, while entertaining company, or while washing dishes after a meal.

- *When in doubt, choose to say "I love you" instead of backing off.*

  If you hear yourself wondering whether you should say "I love you," go ahead and say it. Why not? The risk of something bad happening is small, and the likelihood of something good occurring is high. It's

---

**SMART START**

I love you here. I
  love you now.
I love being on
  your side.

Telling another
  person that you
  are here for them,

Right now in the
  present, and that
  you know you are

Blessed to love
  them, gives them
  the freedom to

Love back, and
  gives both of you
  the power

To move through
  life as a team,
  finding your

Way together.

usually worth the risk, especially when you are training yourself to say "I love you" regularly.

- *Write "I love you" on your notes to your partner.*

    This is an excellent way to vary your routine while helping your brain get used to professing your love. "I've gone to the store. I'll be back by 1:00. I love you."

- *Always end your phone calls with "I love you."*

    If you make this a ritual, every phone conversation will end on a positive note.

## Don't

- *Ever assume that your partner doesn't need to hear the words "I love you."*

    Of course he or she needs to hear those words. Everybody does.

- *Wait until your partner says it first.*

    This is a huge mistake because you're giving all the control to your partner. Besides, "I love you, too" isn't as strong as "I love you."

- *Insist that your partner return the compliment, or keep score of how many times your partner says "I love you" to you.*

    It's certainly great when you receive an "I love you" every time you give one. But don't make that a condition or a demand. Say "I love you" to your partner because it's a nice gift to give without expecting a gift in return. Think of saying "I love you" as giving a birthday gift rather than a Christmas gift exchange.

- *Ever go a day without saying "I love you."*

    Remember, the goal is to develop a positive habit. Habits only develop with repetition. That's why saying "I love you" three times a day is so important. Once a day is the absolute minimum. If you go a whole day without saying "I love you," you simply will not train your brain enough to maintain this behavior.

- *Wait until just the right or perfect time.*

    The right time is right now. The longer you wait, and the more conditions you place on saying "I love you," the less likely you are ever to say it.

- *Think that saying "I love you" is only "real" if it is done spontaneously.*
  Saying "I love you" counts even when you have to think about it. It counts even when it doesn't come naturally.

- *Expect magic or miracles. Saying "I love you" won't resolve all your conflicts.*
  But saying "I love you" helps develop trust, rapport, and caring that will help you discuss your conflicts in a loving way.

- *Automatically connect saying "I love you" with sex.*
  Be careful not to say these words only when you're trying to seduce your partner. "I love you" is not the same as "I want you."

- *Stop practicing until you've developed a firm habit of saying "I love you."*
  Don't take an "Okay, I get the idea, so I don't have to keep practicing" attitude after two or three days. It takes a long time to develop a positive habit. Keep at it until you hear the words "I love you" coming out of your mouth without having to make a conscious decision to say them.

Which of the items on the "Do" list are most important for you to remember? Write them down here. It's okay to change them slightly to put them in your own words.

_____

_____

_____

Which of the items on the "Don't" list are most important for you to remember? Write them down here. It's okay to change them slightly to put them in your own words.

_____

_____

_____

How many times have you said "I love you" to your partner today? ____

Starting tomorrow, write down the number of times you say "I love you" each day for one week.

Day 1: ____    Day 2: ____    Day 3: ____    Day 4: ____

Day 5: ____    Day 6: ____    Day 7: ____

# Say "I love you" ten times to your partner

The phrase "I love you" is powerful. As noted in the introduction, that one sentence means many things, such as:

You are special.

You give meaning to my life.

I think of you often.

I want to make you happy.

You are a wonderful friend.

I can talk to you about anything.

I have a feeling of warmth, closeness, and familiarity with you.

I would grieve if I lost you.

> **SMART TIP**
>
> *Habits are first cobwebs, then cables.*
> —SPANISH PROVERB

Perhaps you can think of other meanings for "I love you." If so, write them down here.

_____

_____

_____

However, simply translating "I love you" into all these phrases is like defining a diamond by its number of facets. True, each facet might sparkle and shine on its own, but you have to look at the entire gem to fully appreciate it. *"I love you" is so important that you must say those exact words, clearly and distinctly, to your partner.* There is no substitute.

SMART TIP

Notice how one moment is different from another, even though the words stay the same.

These two exercises will help both you and your partner feel the full power of the phrase "I love you."

For the first exercise, please do the following:

1. Find two comfortable chairs and position yourselves so you can look at each other and make eye contact.

2. Decide who will go first. You'll both get a turn.

3. The first person says slowly, "I love you," noticing his or her feelings. The other person takes in those words without comment, then pauses for several seconds.

4. The first person continues to say "I love you" nine more times, pausing after each time for several seconds so that both partners can notice their feelings.

5. It's very important that neither partner add any additional words. The strength of "I love you" will only be diluted by "Really, I do"; "Do you believe me?"; "I know you do"; and so on.

6. Take a break for a minute or two. Then switch roles and repeat.

For the second exercise, you will alternate saying "I love you." (1) Have one partner say "I love you" five times in a row. Pause. (2) The other person replies with "I love you" (not "I love you, too"). (3) Switch roles so that the second partner says "I love you" first five times, followed by the first partner.

If you are doing these exercises alone, find a picture of someone you love and try saying "I love you" to that picture ten times. The person can be your partner, a good friend, a parent—anyone who is deserving of your love (i.e., not any old lover with whom you are hoping to reunite).

# Challenge the old, cold thoughts that keep you from saying "I love you"

Rafael loves Miranda. But he never tells her so. Why? Because he grew up in a family in which men don't express any emotion except anger. Even now, in his thirties, he thinks he'd be laughed at if anybody ever heard him proclaim his love.

Shelby loves Aaron. But she keeps that knowledge to herself. She thinks telling Aaron about her love would give him power over her.

People have all kinds of reasons for not saying "I love you." They usually take the form of, "Something bad will happen if I say that." The bad result will come from their partner, family members, or the general community. In other words, they expect some form of punishment for saying "I love you." Now, occasionally they may be right. Sometimes one's partner responds to "I love you" with meanness ("Well, I don't love you") or other people do make fun of the speaker ("Oh, Rafael's going soft"). But nothing bad would happen most of the times people stop themselves from saying "I love you." Actually, good things usually follow from saying those words: hugs, smiles, nice words back.

**23**

So then what really keeps most people from saying "I love you"? The answer is old, negative, irrational thoughts. For instance, Rafael is convinced that people will laugh at him if he says he loves Miranda. But what people? And why would that stop him when it's just the two of them at home talking with each other? And where did Shelby come up with the idea that her saying "I love you" to Aaron gives him power?

Years ago a comic book character said, "We have met the enemy and he is us." That's exactly what we're saying here. Nine times out of ten, the person who keeps you from saying "I love you" is you.

Cognitive therapists label thoughts like Rafael's and Shelby's "irrational." But let's call them "cold thoughts" here. A cold thought is any thought you have that discourages you from saying something loving, caring, or nice to your partner. The opposite of cold thoughts, of course, are "warm thoughts." A warm thought is any thought you have that encourages you to say something loving, caring, or nice to your partner. The idea, then, is to kick out the cold thoughts from your brain while adding some warm thoughts. This substitution process will help you both say "I love you" more often and feel better while saying it. You will need to take three basic steps in order to substitute warm thoughts for cold ones.

## Step One: Identify Your Cold Thoughts

You can't challenge those old, cold thoughts until you know what they are. We'll list several possibilities below, but you are a unique individual with unique thoughts, so only you know your cold thoughts. Please add them to the list as you think of them. You might want to go back to the times you remember stopping yourself from saying "I love you" and ask yourself what thoughts stopped you from saying those words. Those are your cold thoughts.

Here are some common cold thoughts. Are any of them familiar? If so, please check them off.

\_\_\_\_ I'm too shy to say "I love you."

\_\_\_\_ I'm too proud to say "I love you."

\_\_\_\_ I'm too stubborn to say "I love you."

\_\_\_\_ I'll get hurt if I say "I love you" (How? _____

_____ )

\_\_\_\_ I would feel foolish if I said "I love you."

\_\_\_\_ Men don't say things like "I love you."

\_\_\_\_ When I told people I loved them in the past I got hurt, so now I won't say it again.

\_\_\_\_ I'd be giving my partner power over me if I admitted I love him [her].

\_\_\_\_ I wasn't raised to say "I love you," so I can't say it now.

\_\_\_\_ I won't say "I love you" because that would make me feel too dependent or vulnerable.

\_\_\_\_ _____.

\_\_\_\_ _____.

\_\_\_\_ _____.

\_\_\_\_ _____.

## Step Two: Challenge Your Cold Thoughts

Ask yourself this question: What about this cold thought feels old, outdated, unreasonable, irrational, or just plain ridiculous? For example, a challenge to the cold thought "I'm too proud to say 'I love you'" might be that love is not about pride at all. It's about caring, nurturing, bonding, closeness, and connection. Pride has nothing to do with love, so why let it stop you? Why doesn't that cold thought make sense anymore in your life?

Can you come up with a challenge to each of the cold thoughts you have identified?

Cold thought: _____

Challenge: _____

_____

Cold thought: _____

Challenge: _____

_____

Cold thought: _____

Challenge: _____

_____

## Step Three: Substitute Warm Thoughts for Cold Thoughts

The basic formula is this: Instead of my old, cold thought, namely

_____,

I choose to think a new, warm thought, namely _____

_____.

These new, warm thoughts should be more than sensible. They must also feel right to you. If they don't, you won't use them. So take the time to come up with warm thoughts that will really help you say "I love you" more frequently.

Cold thought: _____

Warm thought: _____

Cold thought: _____

Warm thought: _____

Cold thought: _____

Warm thought: _____

Keep track of your old, cold thoughts. They have a way of sneaking back into your brain. Meanwhile, keep reminding yourself about your new thoughts. They need to be repeated frequently for them to feel right.

# Say "I love you" with no strings attached: Be careful of your expectations

"Honey, I love you." There, now I've said it. That means you owe me something. So:

Tell me you love me, too.

How about a kiss?

Pay attention to me.

Be nice to me.

At least smile or say thank you.

These expectations would be fine if love operated on a simple exchange model: "I'll scratch your back if you scratch mine." Indeed, many human activities do fit that model. I'll trade one Mickey Mantle card for two Duke Sniders. I'll fix your broken sink for $250. I'll take the kids to the zoo tomorrow if you watch them today. But saying "I love you" is different. It works better to treat it as a gift, a present to your partner that you give with no strings attached.

Why? There are two main reasons. The first is that expectations often lead to disappointment. The second is that expectations often produce resentment.

Here's what we mean when we say that expectations often lead to disappointment. One day Joe was feeling a little lonely. He wanted some attention and affection from his girlfriend, Pam. He figured that he'd just tell her he loved her. That would surely get her attention. But Pam was busy at the time, studying for an important civil service exam. She barely acknowledged his comment. Joe didn't like her response at all. Here's what he told Pam: "I just said I love you and all you did was nod your head. You didn't even smile. You didn't say that you love me, too. No kiss. No hug. You didn't talk with me. So forget it. I'm not going to do that again!" Joe's mistake is that he thinks Pam owes him something just because he said he loves her. But there is no eleventh commandment that says someone must respond to "I love you" with "I love you, too" or anything else. Joe set himself up for a major disappointment by expecting too much from his partner. Then he turned around and blamed her for it instead of himself.

The second problem is that expectations often produce resentment. Let's go back to Joe and Pam. Same scene. But this time when Joe says, "I love you," Pam rolls her eyes, sighs deeply, slowly closes her book, and turns to Joe. "Okay, Joe," she says wearily, "what do you want from me now?" Then she spends an hour with him, all the while really wanting to study. Pam is building up resentment: "Joe is so selfish. He only thinks about himself. He always wants something from me even when he acts loving." She'll probably start studying even more as a way to avoid contact with him.

The moral of this story is obvious. Say "I love you" with no strings attached. Expect nothing. Demand nothing. Take anything nice that comes back your way as an unexpected treat.

Expecting nothing turns "I love you" into an act of generosity. You are freely giving love to your partner. That's a wonderful gift, probably the best present you could ever offer.

Do you recognize yourself in the story about Joe and Pam? How much are you like Joe, expecting too much from your partner when you say "I love you" or act nice in any other way?

Not at all _____    A little _____    A lot _____

How much are you like Pam, building up resentments because you sense that your partner's "I love you" or kind actions are really demands for your attention?

Not at all _____        A little _____        A lot _____


Please write below a paragraph that begins with the phrase "_____ _____, when I think of saying 'I love you' to you with no strings attached, I feel _____." Include any expectations or demands you've made when saying "I love you" to your current partner or past partners. Write about what those expectations say about you as a person. See if you can figure out how to give your partner your love as an entirely free gift.


_____, when I think of saying "I love you" to you with no strings attached, I feel _____

_____

_____

_____

_____

# Learn why you have trouble saying "I love you"

"I love you" is a wonderful phrase to say to your partner. Nevertheless, many people have blocks against saying it. Some come from the distant past—your family of origin. Others come from the more recent past— such as a love gone badly, which lessened your ability to trust. Still others are immediate—it may have been difficult for you to say "I love you" today because you were angry at your partner.

Blocks against expressing love do tend to follow certain definite, predictable patterns. They relate to what are called Adult Attachment Styles. Each attachment style (there are four in all: Secure, Dismissive, Preoccupied, and Fearful) reflects everything a person has learned about bonding with others. How safe is it to love? How scary? Will people accept me or reject me when I ask for their love? Can I trust the people I love to stick around or will they eventually abandon me? Is all this love stuff even worth the bother or am I better off just taking care of myself?

No single attachment style perfectly describes any one person. You may feel Secure one day, Fearful the next. You may have been Preoccupied with your former lover but Dismissive with your current partner. Still, you probably gravitate more toward one style than the others.

Three of the four attachment styles sometimes make saying "I love you" difficult. Please look over the table below that describes the four patterns of adult attachment.

SMART THOUGHT

Have you ever noticed that people who feel safe and secure are generous with their love, caring, and affection? Let yourself be a generous partner today.

*Adult Attachment Styles*

### Secure

I feel loved and loving.

My family feels like a safe place to me.

I trust the people who are close to me.

I am usually comfortable when alone.

I am usually comfortable with others.

*It feels natural and easy for me to say "I love you."*

### Preoccupied

I worry a lot about what others think of me.

I expect to be rejected or abandoned by the people I love.

I give a lot to others but often think that people don't give back much to me.

I seem to want more closeness than people are willing to give me.

*Saying "I love you" makes me feel very vulnerable.*

### Dismissive

I value independence a lot, even in close relationships.

I don't much want people to depend on me, and I don't want to depend on others.

I get uncomfortable around people who are very emotional or needy.

People should be able to stand on their own two feet.

*Saying "I love you" often feels like a chore or an obligation to me.*

### Fearful

I don't believe I'm worth loving.

I don't trust others very much.

I want to be deeply loved but doubt it will ever happen.

Sometimes I feel I can't count on anybody, including myself.

*I'm just too afraid of rejection to risk saying "I love you."*

Now please answer these questions.

Which of the four attachment styles generally fits you best with regard to your history of close relationships? _____

_____

Second best? _____

Which of the four attachment styles generally fits you best with regard to your current relationship? _____
Second best? _____

Which single statement from any of the four lists best describes you?

_____

Why? _____

_____

_____

Which of the four statements in italics best describes your ability to tell your partner that you love him or her? _____

_____

Why? _____

_____

_____

Which attachment style do you think best describes your partner?

_____

Which single statement do you think best describes your partner?

_____

Which single italicized statement do you think best describes your partner?

_____

(Remember, these are your best guesses. You may want to check them out with him or her.)

By now you may be recognizing where your particular blocks against saying "I love you" are coming from.

You probably don't have many blocks if you are basically Secure. But of course nobody feels totally secure all of the time. So check out the other three styles for information on why you occasionally have trouble expressing love.

You probably shy away from telling your partner you love him or her if you are Dismissive because you fear that expressing love will take away some of your independence and freedom. *You can get better at saying "I love you" by realizing that you and only you are in control of what you say.* Telling your partner that you feel love doesn't put your life in that person's hands.

From time to time you may become Preoccupied around the question of whether your partner loves you. When that happens you may demand love but forget to express yours. Or you may say "I love you," but with a big string attached that sounds like this: "I love you. Now I insist that you say you love me." *You can get better at telling your partner about your love by getting outside yourself for a while.* In other words, you need to learn how to say "I love you" without expecting or demanding an immediate reply in kind.

When you feel Fearful you just want to run away from the whole love trap. Certainly you want love in your life, but at these times you feel pretty hopeless about ever getting it. You don't tell your partner about your love because you are too scared of his or her rejection or disinterest. *You can get better at saying "I love you" by fighting the belief that you're not worth loving.* Yes, telling your partner "I love you" is risky. But not expressing your love isn't getting you what you most want in life, is it?

So now what? First, we suggest that you take the time to reflect on what you have just learned about yourself. You might want to write a page or two about how the attachment style you most identify with has affected your ability to show love to others (and to take it in). Some memories might come up while you are writing about past incidents and relationships that will help you understand how you relate to your partner. Remember as you think and write, though, that you are not a prisoner of the past. Next, we suggest that you share this information with your partner if the two of you are working together on this workbook. Third, please continue to the next exercise: "Saying 'I love you': Getting started and keeping going."

You can begin your writing about your attachment styles here.

_____

_____

_____

_____

_____

_____

_____

_____

# Saying "I love you": Getting started and keeping going

We discussed three blocks to intimacy in the last exercise. *Dismissiveness* leads people to avoid close relationships altogether in favor of taking care of themselves. The phrase "I love you" often seems useless and even a sign of weakness to the dismisser. *Preoccupation* puts the focus on the other person—the goal is to make one's partner express his or her love. Meanwhile, *fearfulness* makes people retreat from all forms of intimacy because they become too scared of rejection to risk involvement.

Fortunately, people are not stuck in one attachment style forever. Indeed, research has shown that people are likely to move toward becoming more *secure* over time than dismissive, preoccupied, or fearful. And secure is a great place to be in terms of saying "I love you." The more secure you feel, the easier it is both to tell your partner you love him or her and to take in that person's love.

So, if you aren't quite there yet (or want to feel secure in your love more often), what can you do? The answer lies in this story told to Ron by a teacher he had years ago. This man was an expert in behavior modification techniques for couples. He was excellent at helping partners develop more loving and caring behaviors. But this teacher had a complaint. He found it much easier to get people to agree to do the dishes three times a week than to get them to agree to tell their partner "I love you." The reason, he

> **SMART SAYING**
>
> *There is no remedy for love but to love more.*
>
> —HENRY DAVID THOREAU

**39**

said, was that many people believed a phrase like "I love you" should always be spoken spontaneously. Planning ahead and committing to saying "I love you" five times a day to their partner would feel phony and insincere to these people. They wanted to wait until they really felt like saying it before they did. Well, that reluctance amazed and frustrated Ron's teacher. He argued that a person could wait forever to be inspired to say "I love you." Meanwhile, the distance between partners keeps building as they wait and wait and wait. *Practice* is what they need, not spontaneity, he said.

We think that teacher is correct. The more often you tell your partner you love him or her, the easier it will become. After all, what doesn't become easier with practice? Furthermore, by stating your love, you are helping both yourself and your partner become more secure. You are moving your entire relationship toward security and away from dismissiveness, preoccupation, and fearfulness.

But what about spontaneity? Shouldn't that have a place? Certainly. And it will. *After* you practice saying "I love you," though, not before. That's because the more you practice saying "I love you," the easier it will get, and once it gets easier to say, it will also become more spontaneous. Ask yourself, for example, who is more likely to spontaneously decide to take a five-mile bike ride—someone who jumps on a bike maybe twice a year or someone who rides almost every day? The same principle applies here. The more you practice saying "I love you" nonspontaneously, the more you will begin saying "I love you" without having to think about it ahead of time.

Let's handle another objection to regularly saying "I love you." Perhaps you are thinking that you can't mean it all the time if you say it five times a day rather than saving it for moments of special closeness. Well, we think that's wrong. In fact, we believe that you will mean it more and more when you do tell your partner frequently about your love. Think about it this way. There are *two* listeners every time you say "I love you" out loud—your partner and yourself. Your brain hears you speak that magic phrase. It hears you profess your love. Imagine your brain saying to itself, "Oh, I'm saying I love him [her], so I guess I do."

Finally, we're not suggesting you fake feelings of love here. It won't do much good to just say the words if they have no meaning to you. We're encouraging you to practice saying "I love you" because we believe you really do love your partner. So put some emotion into your words. Vary your tone of voice. Have a little fun with this experiment. But whatever you do, keep saying "I love you" so that you become more comfortable with that phrase.

There's a simple lesson in all this talk. You have to *start* saying "I love you." You have to *keep* saying "I love you." You have to *practice* saying "I love you." That's the best way to build and keep love in your life.

We're going to assume at this point that you want to increase the number of times you say "I love you" to your partner. If so, there are two ways to do it.

## 1. The Scientific Approach

Pick two days a week (one weekday, one weekend day) to collect your "I love you" baseline data. That means noticing how often you tell your partner you love him or her before you start increasing the number. Don't think about adding to this number yet. The idea is to get a good idea of how often you usually say "I love you." Whatever the number, whether it's zero or twelve, you may still want to increase it.

Day One (weekday): How many times did you say "I love you" to your partner? _____

Day Two (weekend day): How many times did you say "I love you" to your partner? _____

Set a goal, such as saying "I love you" to your partner at least three times a day on weekdays and at least six times a day on weekends.

My goal is to say "I love you" to my partner _____ times a day.

Work your way toward that goal. Start by adding one "I love you" a day to your baseline (say, by going from zero to one or from three to four). Then gradually increase your target number so that within a couple of weeks you are regularly saying "I love you" to your partner several times a day.

This first day I'll try to say "I love you" to my partner _____ times.

Tomorrow I'll try to say "I love you" to my partner _____ times.

Next week I'll try to say "I love you" to my partner at least _____ times a day.

Keep practicing. Remember that the real goal here is to keep saying "I love you" day after day. So every month or so go back to checking out your baseline on one weekday and one weekend day. If you are keeping up the pace, consider challenging yourself to add an extra "I love you" or two to your routine. If you have slid back toward your original numbers, don't be discouraged. Ask yourself how that may have happened and renew your commitment to saying "I love you" more often.

One month from my start date I said "I love you" to my partner _____ times.

Two months from my start date I said "I love you" to my partner _____ times.

Three months from my start date I said "I love you" to my partner _____ times.

## 2. The "Oh, What the Heck, I Might as Well Take the Plunge" Method

This is a lot simpler but may not work as well in the long run. You just make a commitment to yourself, right now, that beginning today you will say "I love you" to your partner at least five times a day (or six or eight—you pick the number). And then do it. But you still need to keep track and check up on yourself every few days. Remember, it's one thing to say you're going to change and another to actually do it.

Oh, what the heck, I might as well make that commitment to tell my partner I love him [her] at least _____ times, beginning today.

It's one week later. How am I doing? _____

_____ .

It's one month later. How am I doing? _____

_____ .

It's three months later. How am I doing? _____

_____ .

One last warning: just because you are saying "I love you" to your partner does not obligate him or her to say it to you. Don't turn a gift into a demand.

# Explore nonverbal ways to say "I love you"

Yolanda tells her partner, Jermaine, "I love you." However, she speaks in a monotone, leans back, looks away, and seems bored. Her verbal message is "I love you." But her nonverbal message is "I don't really mean what I'm saying."

If you were Jermaine, which message would you believe? Well, if you're like most people, the answer is the nonverbal message. Study after study has demonstrated a simple truth: when people are given a choice between believing two contradictory messages delivered simultaneously, one verbally and the other nonverbally, the one they believe will be the nonverbal one. So, if you plan on telling your partner about your intense and undying love, you need to make sure your nonverbal message matches your words.

The phrase "nonverbal communication" refers to many things, especially:

• Vocalisms (soft to loud tone of voice, monotone to varied rhythm, etc.)

• Touch (soft to firm)

• Body posture and movement (leaning toward to leaning away, completely still to constantly active)

• Eye contact (none to steady and direct)

SMART TIP

Start with your eyes. Can you say "I love you" attractively with your toes?

Here's a simple formula for making sure your "I love you" message comes across loud and clear on all channels: (1) say the words clearly and directly, (2) speak in a quiet tone of voice, (3) make direct and "soft" (not glaring) eye contact, (4) lean toward your partner, and (5) (sometimes) touch or hold your partner gently.

Now, some people have an easier time at this than others. If you have a Secure attachment style (see page 34) or if you are generally extroverted or grew up in a demonstrative family, chances are pretty good that your non-verbal communication is spontaneous, rich, and varied. On the other hand, if your attachment style is Dismissive or Fearful, or if you are intro-verted by nature or grew up in a nondemonstrative household, your non-verbal communication may be muted. Whatever your situation, though, it's important that you get your message across to your partner. So keep the formula above in mind as you speak.

So far we've been writing about how nonverbal communication com-plements verbal communication. But sometimes you may want to express your love to your partner without using any words at all. Here are a few ways to do that, starting with the most direct.

- Mouth the words "I love you" from across the room.

- Use nonverbal humor: grab your chest and fall over in a loving swoon; draw a heart on the steamy bathroom mirror.

- Just look at your partner with a soft, loving gaze.

- Listen to your partner as if hearing his or her words were the single most important thing you could ever do.

- Notice the small things that relax, comfort, or calm your partner and offer them when needed. A timely cup of tea, a hug, a warm blanket, turning the lights on so he or she can read better—over time these caring acts will become associated with love.

Here are a few questions for you about your use of nonverbal commu-nication to say "I love you."

Which of the ways to say "I love you" nonverbally that we listed most appeals to you?

_____

_____ .

How important for you is it to receive nonverbal "I love you" messages from your partner?

_____

_____ .

Why?

_____

_____ .

How important do you think it is for your partner to receive nonverbal "I love you" messages from you?

_____

_____ .

Why?

_____

_____ .

What nonverbal ways of saying "I love you" do you think work best with your partner?

_____

_____ .

How could you improve your nonverbal communication pattern so you can better say "I love you" without words to your partner?

_____

_____ .

# Say "I love you" with creativity, humor, and imagination

There is something absurd about being in love. Loving somebody is romantic, silly, funny, ridiculous, foolish, joyful, pleasurable, bittersweet, weird, and wonderful—often all at the same time. So why make saying "I love you" such a serious thing? Why not play with the idea of love, exploring some lighter ways to tell your partner how much you care?

That's where creativity, humor, and imagination enter the scene. Fortunately, being creative about saying "I love you" doesn't call for a lot of hard work or money. You will probably need to set aside some time to gear up your imagination, though. You'll also have to think about what kind of play appeals to your partner. You'll want your partner to feel pleasantly surprised and a little giggly, not shocked or uncomfortable, by your creative efforts.

Sometimes little things work great. For instance, you could simply place a sweet note in your partner's purse or briefcase. Or pick up a favorite dessert as an unexpected treat. But maybe you'd be willing to go a bit further down the road of creativity. That calls for thinking outside the box. Ask yourself this question: *How can I tell my partner I love him [her] in unexpected ways?* Your immediate goal should be to pleasantly surprise your partner. Longer term, the goal is to keep the love between you feeling fresh, playful, joyful, and spontaneous.

SMART TIP

Taking "I love you" out of its everyday box reminds us how true it is. Did you know that it is not uncommon for rocks to be found heart-shaped? An "I Love You" rock is an old rock— and never trite.

Here are a few ways in which you could experiment.

How many types of voices could you use to say "I love you"? How about these.

A giant's booming voice

A "breaking news" voice

A southern drawl

A New England accent

A sweet voice

A Donald Duck quack

A telephone receptionist voice

A cheerleader's call

What kind of physical movements could accompany saying "I love you"? Here are a few possibilities.

Falling over on the floor

Kneeling

Standing on your head

Arms outstretched

Pretending to hold a microphone

Dancing

Jumping up and down

Hopping

Waddling

Where could you say "I love you"? Think of places and situations you would not usually associate with saying "I love you" and then say it anyhow.

While changing the baby's diaper

In the midst of an argument

In the bathtub

In the middle of dinner

At the library

Before, during, or after sex (whenever you are least likely to proclaim your love)

While discussing finances

While jogging together

While watching TV

At 3:00 A.M. when you are both awake

When you are repairing the roof

Put these three areas together and you get a wealth of possibilities.

| Voice | Movement | Place/Situation |
|---|---|---|
| Donald Duck quack | Waddling | In the bathtub |
| Giant's booming voice | Arms outstretched | While jogging together |
| "Breaking-news" voice | Dancing | In the midst of an argument |
| Southern drawl | Standing on your head | At the library |

Now it's your turn. Fill in the blanks:

| Voice | Movement | Place/Situation |
|---|---|---|
| _____ | _____ | _____ |
| _____ | _____ | _____ |
| _____ | _____ | _____ |
| _____ | _____ | _____ |

The rest is up to you. Enjoy!

# Praise helps your partner feel loved

We've done a lot of marriage counseling, and one thing we've noticed is that troubled couples spend more time criticizing each other than saying anything nice. Their relationships have gradually gravitated toward attack and defense, shaming, hostility, negativity, and disrespect. They look for what's wrong about each other and always find it. They would be much happier with each other if only they could turn that habit around and begin noticing and commenting on what their partners do that pleases them.

You may already be thinking to yourself that people see what they are looking for. And you're absolutely correct. That means we'll start seeing more good in our partners exactly to the extent that we train ourselves to look for the good.

You may also be thinking that you get what you respond to. And again you are correct. People who comment almost exclusively on their partner's faults actually are encouraging their partners to get worse rather than better. For example, if you tell me over and over how sloppy I am, I can almost guarantee you that I will get sloppier. On the other hand, if you pay attention to the times I clean up around the house and tell me that you appreciate my efforts, chances are I will keep picking things up.

People need to be praised. Your partner needs to be praised. It helps

**SMART TIP**

Praise your partner to someone else within your partner's hearing.

53

him or her feel accepted, respected, wanted, and competent. So make sure that you *give praise at least four or five times for every critical remark.* You can train yourself to do this if you are willing to look for things to appreciate and then tell your partner about them.

If you come from a family in which praise was seldom given, it probably doesn't feel natural to give praise to anyone, including your partner. But you definitely can learn this skill. And if you do, your partner will almost certainly feel more loved.

Here is a partial list of things to praise. The examples we give have to do with your relationship.

*Deeds.* The nice things your partner does that make your lives better. Picking up around the house, planning a special meal, painting the closet, training the dog . . .

*Effort.* The energy your partner expends for the sake of your relationship. Taking extra time to be with you, reading this book, working so hard, really listening to you . . .

*Thoughtfulness.* The special ways your partner shows caring to you and others. Little things like bringing you a cup of tea, noticing when you're feeling blue, writing you a special note . . .

*Creativity.* The playful activities or new ideas your partner comes up with that help keep your relationship alive. A surprise gift, a silly joke, a sexy wink, an idea for a new hobby or place to go together . . .

*Generosity.* The ways your partner goes out of his or her way to show caring. Staying up with the kids when you're too tired, asking about your day before talking about his or her own, performing acts of kindness . . .

*Appearance.* The uniquely beautiful aspects of your partner's style and appearance. His or her nice bracelet, beautiful eyes, wonderful smile, great-looking coat . . .

*Individuality.* Special aspects of your partner's character and personality that stand out. His or her honesty, caring, intelligence, thoughtfulness, strength, optimism, playfulness, gentleness . . .

Giving praise is a wonderful thing. However, we want to caution you against making two common mistakes.

1. Don't ever follow praise with the word *but*, as in "Sal, I liked making love with you this morning, but . . ." That word *but* always announces that you are about to say something critical to your partner. Following praise with criticism is like following a kiss with a punch in the nose.

2. Don't expect or demand to receive praise from the person you praise. Make your praise a gift that comes with no strings attached.

Please write your answers to these questions in the spaces below.

What kind of family did you grow up in with regard to giving praise? In general, was your family generous with praise? Conservative with praise? How often did your parents praise each other? How critical were they of each other? How praising or critical were they of you?

_____

_____

_____

_____

_____

_____

How has that background affected your ability to give praise in your relationships?

_____

_____

_____

What kinds of praise are you good at giving?

_____

_____

_____

What kinds of praise do you need to work on giving so you can do so more often?

_____

_____

_____

Can you think of any praise you have given your partner in the last twenty-four hours? What did you praise?

_____

_____

_____

How about criticism in the last twenty-four hours? What did you criticize?

_____

_____

_____

What three things about your partner can you think of immediately that you could praise?

1. _____

2. _____

3. _____

Now write down three more things to praise, this time taking the time to think about things you may not have noticed before.

1. _____

2. _____

3. _____

When next will you tell your partner these things you appreciate about him or her?

_____

# Write a love letter to your partner

Why do so many couples falling in love exchange love letters? There are many reasons.

- Writing lets them express things that are sometimes hard to say out loud.

- Writing helps them think about what they really like about each other.

- Writing brings out their romantic side.

- Writing helps them feel connected with each other even when they are apart.

- Writing helps them tell their partners who they are and how they got that way.

- Writing love letters is a way of saying "I love you" that just feels good.

- Receiving love letters reassures them that their partners are thinking about them.

Exchanging love letters is a traditional part of courtship. But, once people make the commitment to live together, letter writing often ends. Who thinks about writing a letter to the person sitting right next to them at the

**SMART SAYING**

*One word frees us of all the weight and pain of life: that word is love.*

—SOPHOCLES

breakfast table? Ten-page-long mushy love letters gradually morph into practical little notes: "Honey, please pick up bread and milk on the way home tonight."

Our suggestion is simple enough. Take the time to *write your partner a love letter at least once a month*. No, it doesn't have to be ten pages long. Two or three will do just fine. But it does have to be a little mushy, meaning that you write about your love for your partner, your feelings, your hopes and dreams, and your fears and worries rather than about your pension, the children's arguments, or your lower back pain.

Probably the hardest thing about writing a love letter, if you haven't written one for a while, is getting started. It might help you to think of writing a love letter like getting ready to cook up a particularly delicious dish. First you collect your basic instruments: pen, paper, et cetera. Then you gather your core ingredients: the most important ways you can tell your partner you love him or her. Finally, you spice up the dish with a little humor, a lot of warmth, and, most important, your own style of sharing love. Just remember as you plan your dish that the goal is to make a meal that both you and your partner find tasty. So make sure you throw in some words and thoughts that will be particularly pleasing to your partner.

Here's where we come in. We'll supply some of the basic ingredients for your letter, in the form of suggestions about what you might want to include. Each ingredient is followed by an example. Realize, though, that you are the chef in charge of this particular feast. Use any or all of the ingredients we offer, selecting those that help you best express your love for your partner. Add or subtract as you like. Write the letter in your style. Don't worry about getting it perfect. Just write.

**Smart Move**

If you can't write a love letter, write a love limerick.

### Suggested Ingredients for a Love Letter

- That you like the way your partner expresses himself or herself ("You say what you think so clearly")
- Things your partner does that make him or her special ("You take wonderful pictures")
- What you find especially physically attractive about your partner ("You have beautiful blue-green eyes")

- That you still choose your partner ("Of all the people in the world, I want you most")

- How fortunate you are to have made a life together ("You've made my world complete")

- What you've learned from your partner ("I've learned how to care about others from you")

- How you've let your partner into your life ("Only you know that I am afraid of people")

- That your love is special ("I never thought I could be this much in love with anyone")

- That you will be true and faithful ("I want to be with you the rest of my life")

- That you will help your partner ("I know you love flowers, so let's plant a garden")

- How your love is a spiritual union ("I believe God has joined us together")

- How much you enjoy making love with your partner ("You are a great kisser")

- That your partner matters to you ("You mean so much to me")

- How your partner's love comforts you ("I feel calm and peaceful around you")

- Your appreciation of your partner's sense of humor ("You make me smile")

- That you think of your partner often ("I find myself thinking of you all the time")

So have you made your selections? Which items from the list do you want to include in your love letter? We suggest you choose at least five and see how that goes. Experiment with these ingredients for a while. Then, if you want to keep writing, select another five. Don't throw in too much stuff, though. Think about which items on the list mean the most to you and your partner. You can always write another letter in a couple of weeks using a few more ingredients from the list.

Be careful to avoid all criticism or negativity. Do not ask your partner to change in any way. A love letter is a celebration of your relationship.

By the way, this is definitely not a no-send letter. You'll want to hand deliver your letter to your partner, or maybe put it in a special place for him or her to discover while you're away.

# Share your deepest hopes, dreams, and yearnings with your partner

"Sure, we spend a lot of time together. We play with the kids. We watch TV. But we never talk about anything serious."

"We talked about everything before we were married. Now we just go about our business."

"We used to dream together. We talked about what we most wanted to do with our lives. But we don't do that anymore."

Are you in a relationship like this? If so, you are missing out on something wonderful: emotional intimacy. Emotional intimacy occurs when one person talks about things that are very important to himself or herself while the other listens very carefully and responds emotionally to the speaker.

Most couples talk about anything and everything during courtship. That's because courtship is a place for dreaming, telling secrets, and sharing feelings. Courting people want to say everything, hear everything. "Tell me about yourself," they say. "You're the most important person in the world." They may talk for hours on end, often about nothing but sometimes about the most private aspects of themselves. They're getting to

SMART THOUGHT

Hope keeps us
    positive;
Yearning keeps us
    looking ahead;
Dreaming gives us
    new energy,
Sharing adds power
    to all these.

**61**

know each other because they have to decide if they want to spend the rest of their lives together. Then they agree to become a couple and *boom*, the discovery phase of the relationship is declared over. It's like a switch goes off. "Okay, now I know who you are and you know who I am. I guess we don't ever have to do that again." Then they get to work raising their family, making a living. Some couples never return to that deep level of intimacy. They say they're just too busy, too tired. Maybe they'll start talking again when the kids are grown. Perhaps during retirement. Possibly sometime in the distant future they will rediscover emotional intimacy. In the meantime, though, people keep growing and changing. Even their hopes and dreams change with time. Unfortunately, if partners don't share these revised dreams, they gradually lose touch with each other. Dreams need to be shared regularly for a relationship to thrive.

There is no better time than right now to reconnect at this deeper level of love. So how do you do that? Well, you have to start talking again about the stuff that really matters to each of you. And one way to do that is to share your deepest hopes, dreams, and yearnings.

Start by taking at least fifteen minutes just by yourself to answer the following questions.

What are my hopes and dreams for the immediate future? (In other words, if you could do whatever you wanted in the next couple of years, what would you want to do?)

_____

_____

_____

When I let myself dream about what I most want to do with my life, here's what I think about:

_____

_____

_____

I hardly ever tell anyone about this, but something I would love to do during my life would be:

_____

_____

_____

Something really important to me that I haven't talked with you about in a long time is:

_____

_____

_____

If I could develop a two-person business or hobby with you, it would be:

_____

_____

_____

Now take your answers to your partner, who perhaps has also answered these questions. Talk about your deepest hopes, dreams, and yearnings. Don't hold back. Don't worry about how impractical your dreams are. Of course they're impractical. That's why they're called dreams. Just talk about them while your partner listens and asks noncritical questions. The idea is to begin dreaming together again.

# Practice intimacy: Saying "I love you" by opening the gates to your private world

You're starting to know someone a little more. You'd like to get closer. But you are a quiet person who keeps a lot inside. Telling someone about yourself doesn't come naturally. The thought of revealing some of your deeper thoughts, feelings, and secrets is scary. On the other hand, your partner has told you some of his or her personal experiences, private information not revealed to just anybody. It felt great to be trusted that way. You're fairly certain you would also feel good if you could just tell your partner more about your life.

Are you ready to take your turn? Are you willing to open the gates to your private world? If so, please read on.

What is *intimacy*? To us, intimacy means two people both sharing their private worlds with each other and deeply respecting each other's disclosures. Intimacy is achieved when each partner takes the risk of sharing secrets and the other responds with love, caring, interest, and acceptance (as opposed to ridicule, disinterest, defensiveness, or attack). Intimacy begins when one person decides, "I'll take a chance by telling you something important about myself" and the other responds, "Go ahead. We're in this together. You can trust me with whatever you tell me. And I'll tell you about myself, too."

We have a model of how people share information about themselves that looks like this:

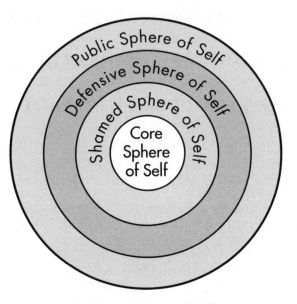

**The Four Spheres of Self**

SMART TIP

You may fear self-disclosure because you think others will criticize or judge you, but think about it. Who is your biggest critic? We'll bet it's you, yourself. Chances are your partner will help you feel better about yourself, not worse, if you open up and talk.

The outer circle is called the Public Sphere of Self. That's the part of ourselves we let everybody see. The public sphere consists mostly of our roles (such as mechanic, wife, mother) and our public image (perhaps always smiling, always optimistic). Sometimes we feel really comfortable with those roles and images. At other times the public sphere feels like a mask we have to wear around people but can't wait to take off.

We call the second circle the Defensive Sphere of Self. That's where we figure out how to keep people away from us, how to keep them from getting too close. Some typical defenses include denial ("I don't know what you're talking about"), refusal ("I won't talk about it"), addictions that take people away from their emotional pain, anger designed to keep others distant, and numbness that helps keep people from feeling bad. Note that some of these defenses don't only keep others distant, they even stop people from getting to know themselves better. The message of the defensive sphere is "Don't go there." That order may be given to yourself as well as to others.

The third circle represents the Shamed Sphere of Self. Shame is the sense that there is something wrong with one at the very center of one's being. The phrases that often go with shame include "I am no good," "I am not good enough," "I am unlovable," "I don't belong," and "I should not exist." Here is where people keep their secrets, especially the kind of information that they would never want the general public to learn. This is the stuff people are definitely not proud about: their long-ago arrest for smoking dope, past relationship or business failures, having dropped out of school—basically anything that they believe would be deeply embarrassing and discrediting if ever made public.

The last circle stands for the Core Sphere of Self. This is a very private place so special that only a cherished few are ever allowed inside. The core self contains one's hopes and dreams, deepest feelings, spirit, and essence. It is only when you reach this place that you can truly answer the question "Who am I?"

Let's return to the concept of intimacy. We believe that intimacy develops between partners as they gradually allow each other to see past their public selves, shut down their defenses, disclose their secrets, and reveal their deepest selves. This process may take days, weeks, months, or years. It usually occurs very powerfully during courtship. However, emotional intimacy isn't something you do just one time with your partner. You can't just get there and stay there. That's because you are always growing and changing. So is your partner. Yesterday's disclosures may have been beautiful and powerful, but they were yesterday's. Intimacy between partners is always growing or dying. The gates to that particular world are always swinging open or shut.

Here is an exercise designed to help you discover things about all four spheres of yourself. Please do it alone. Take your time with it. Then, if your partner is involved in this journey with you, read what you have written out loud to him or her—slowly—so you can notice your feelings. Get some feedback. Then listen without criticism to what your partner has written.

## Your Public Sphere of Self

Write down ten things about yourself that just about everybody knows. This can include your name, gender, and so on.

_____          _____

_____          _____

_____          _____

_____          _____

_____          _____

## Your Defensive Sphere of Self

See if you can answer these questions.

What do I do or say to keep the gates to my inner world closed?

_____

_____

Why do I do that? Why am I reluctant to tell my partner about myself?

_____

_____

## Your Shamed Sphere of Self

Everybody has secrets, deeply personal information that we are very reluctant to share with anyone, even our closest friends. That's normal. We're not going to ask you to put down on paper anything like that. But please complete the following sentences.

When I think about telling my secrets—the things I am ashamed or guilty about—I feel

_____

_____

If I were to tell my partner my secrets, I would need him or her to

_____

_____

If my partner would reveal his or her secrets to me, I would

_____

_____

## Your Core Sphere of Self

First, we're going to ask you to answer one question. The catch is, we're going to ask it ten times. Do the best you can and don't worry if you get stuck for a while.

Who are you? (Try not to answer by listing your roles—mother, office worker, etc.—or anything else from your public sphere of self.)

_____

Who are you? _____

Who are you? _____

Who are you? _____

Who are you? _____

Who are you? _____

Who are you? _____

Who are you? _____

Who are you? _____

Who are you? _____

Now try answering this question five times.

Who are you becoming?    _____

Who are you becoming?    _____

Who are you becoming?    _____

Who are you becoming?    _____

Who are you becoming?    _____

And now see if you can complete this sentence:

_____, there is something about myself I haven't talked about much with you, and I would like to now. It is _____

_____

_____

_____

# Say "I love you" during really hard times

There are two times when remembering to say "I love you" becomes especially important. The first is when things are going very badly between the two of you. The second is when things are going very badly for one or both of you with the rest of the world.

Let's start with troubled times between the two of you. Almost every relationship goes through difficult periods sooner or later. These are the times when you're displeased with almost everything your partner says or does. When everything goes wrong. When you can't understand your partner and he or she can't understand you. When whatever you do as you try to fix things seems only to make them worse. When you find yourself thinking that maybe your life would be better if the two of you separated, even though that's the last thing you really want. You begin wondering if you actually are still in love with your partner, although deep down you know you are.

Saying "I love you" doesn't come naturally during these times. But this is exactly when that statement is most needed. "I love you" is a healing phrase. It helps people get closer, countering the sense of isolation and distance from your partner that accompanies difficult periods. Saying "I love you" is a reminder that even though you don't like what your partner is doing, you still want him or her in your life. Now, of course just saying "I

**SMART SAYING**

*What do we live for, if not to make life less difficult for each other.*
—GEORGE ELIOT

love you" won't solve any problems all by itself. Nor will it always turn things around right away (although sometimes it does indeed do just that). But it will help the two of you feel more hopeful about your relationship. Just make sure that "I love you" is never followed by the word "but," as in, "I love you, but you are wrong [stupid, ridiculous, thoughtless, mean . . . ]."

Then there are the times when very discouraging events happen to one or both of you. A job layoff. A serious illness. A death in the family. Critical financial problems. Serious mental health problems such as anxiety or depression. A distant daughter. A troubled son. That's when you most need an ally in life, someone who will help you get through bad times. Here's what "I love you" means in these situations.

"You're not alone."

"It's tough, but we'll get through it together."

"I'll support you in every way I can."

"We can do this."

"Let me help you."

"It's not the end of the world."

"You can count on me."

We hope that you and your partner are not at a stage in your relationship as we've just described. But if you are, the next exercise could be particularly important. If you're not, think back to the last time you and your partner were having big problems with each other or the world.

When you think about the state of your partnership during this crisis stage, what feelings do or did you have? (Check all that apply.)

| | | | |
|---|---|---|---|
| ___ Anger | ___ Sadness | ___ Despair | ___ Anxiety |
| ___ Loneliness | ___ Emptiness | ___ Shame | ___ Guilt |
| ___ Resentment | ___ Pain | ___ Hurt | ___ Numbness |

What is happening or happened to your ability to say "I love you" during this crisis? (Check the statement that applies.)

\_\_\_\_ Nothing. I still can say "I love you" without any difficulty.

\_\_\_\_ I don't say "I love you" as often as I used to.

\_\_\_\_ I hardly ever say "I love you" anymore.

\_\_\_\_ I say "I love you," but it feels mechanical, without much real feeling.

\_\_\_\_ I say "I love you," but it feels desperate and needy instead of comfortable.

\_\_\_\_ I still say "I love you," but I don't really mean it anymore.

What do or did you most need to think to yourself to get back to saying "I love you" even though things are or were not going well? (Check the statement that applies.)

\_\_\_\_ I love _____ even though right now I'm not very happy with him or her.

\_\_\_\_ _____ is a good person.

\_\_\_\_ I have faith that we're going to make it.

\_\_\_\_ We're in this together.

\_\_\_\_ I refuse to give up on us.

\_\_\_\_ I made a commitment: for better or worse.

\_\_\_\_ We've gotten through tough times before so we can do it again.

\_\_\_\_ This bad stuff is just a stage, but my love is forever.

\_\_\_\_ My life is a lot better with _____ than it would be without him or her.

_____ I won't let anything pull us apart.

_____ It's time to quit playing games and get back to being loving to my partner.

_____ I'm not a quitter.

_____ My love is stronger than anger [sadness, despair, anxiety, loneliness, emptiness, shame, guilt, resentment, pain, hurt, numbness].

_____ Other _____.

Will you let yourself think these thoughts right now if you need them? The next time you get really upset with your partner? The next time you two go through tough times? Will you remind yourself regularly that "I love you" is a sentence that belongs in your daily life no matter what else is happening?

# Don't keep it a secret: Tell others you love your partner

Some people think of love as a very private, very personal thing. Perhaps they just don't like displaying their emotions in public. Possibly they grew up in homes where their parents only displayed their affection behind closed doors. Maybe they even feel a little embarrassed or ashamed, as if it were silly or childish to be in love. The result, at any rate, is the same. These people seldom tell or show others they're in love. Their love remains a carefully guarded secret.

We think that's a mistake. Why? Because it is important that you let the world know that you're in love. There are actually several reasons this is so. First, telling others about your love may help that love grow stronger in your own heart. Saying "I love him [her]" often and to many people usually makes that love feel more real and powerful. Second, telling others about your love is a great way to honor your partner. It lets your partner know that you are proud of being in love with him or her. Third, love thrives when it is celebrated by the entire community. Anniversaries, for example, are times when a group gathers just to appreciate the ongoing love of two people for each other. Fourth, and perhaps the most compelling reason, is that it simply feels good to tell others about your great good fortune. You are in love. That's worth talking about.

**SMART HABIT**

Try "good-mouthing" your partner to someone else at least once a day.

75

No, you don't have to hire a pilot to write the name of your beloved in the sky. You don't have to write a love song and sing it in the rain. (Those aren't bad ideas either, but they are extra-special events.) We're talking about smaller but more frequent conversations with your family, friends, coworkers, and associates in which you mention your love. These are the kinds of conversations in which people normally talk about their partners. Sometimes they become complaint sessions: "My boyfriend is so stupid." "All my wife does is nag, nag, nag." "She's fat." "He's ugly." That's unfortunate. Bad-mouthing your partner only leads to feelings of anger, resentment, and self-pity. On the other hand, telling others what you like about your partner solidifies your love and appreciation.

Basically, we are suggesting that you do two things in these routine conversations. First, use them to let people know you're still in love. Second, tell people what you like and admire about your partner.

So, when's the last time you said something nice about your partner to someone else? _____

To whom were you talking? _____

What did you say? _____

When's the last time you actually said "I love _____" to anyone else? _____

To whom did you say it? _____.

Here's a special exercise. Doing it will help you feel more comfortable telling others about your love.

Please think of one person you will call or speak face-to-face with today. This person should be a good friend—someone you trust, but not your partner or a member of your immediate family. Your goal will be to tell that person about your love for your partner and what you particularly admire about him or her.

Whom have you picked? _____

Go ahead and tell that person that you are doing an assignment in which you tell another person about your love for your partner. Ask if it's okay to do that now. If it is, then start right in. Be prepared with at least three things you especially admire or appreciate about your partner.

The three things I admire or appreciate about my partner that I want to mention are:

1. _____

2. _____

3. _____

Don't just say these things and change the conversation. Give the person who is listening an opportunity to respond. Also, notice your feelings as you talk about your love. Hopefully, you'll see how your love grows when you tell people about it.

# Choosing not to hurt your partner: What not to say in the name of love

Most of the exercises in this book are meant to help readers learn ways to say and do good things for their partners. But we wanted to include at least one exercise on what *not* to say and do. That's because, as you probably know from your own experience, even one particularly rude, insensitive, or mean-spirited outburst can badly damage a relationship. Furthermore, you can't just balance one nasty comment with one nice comment. People simply pay more attention to bad stuff than good. That's one reason the marriage researcher John Gottman recommends a ratio of at least five praising comments for every critical one. But if it basically takes five positive statements to make up for one negative comment, then doesn't it make sense to try not to make that nasty comment in the first place?

Healthy relationships depend on trust as well as love. And one of the most important areas in which trust develops centers on this phrase: *"I know exactly how to hurt you, but I won't."*

Here's what we mean. Say you've been going out with someone for three months. By now your partner has begun to tell you private things. Perhaps he or she was abused as a child. Maybe his or her first relationship ended bitterly. Possibly he or she secretly can't stand a brother or a sister. The point is that your new partner is gradually feeding you information that you could use against him or her. If you're learning all that in the first few months, imagine how much you'll know after three years. After thirty-three years.

Of course you are probably also giving your partner information about yourself. That means you are gradually becoming more vulnerable, so your partner is capable of hurting you, too.

Things are going well between the two of you. But then comes a huge argument about money or spending enough time with each other or sex. You're furious with your partner, and he or she isn't exactly happy with you, either. At that point each of you has a thought process that goes like this:

a. I'm really mad at you.

b. I'm so mad that part of me desperately wants to say or do something that will make you feel awful.

c. I'm tempted, but should I?

And then, the fatal mistake: Sure, why not? I may pay for this later, but right now I'll get that blow in. But what to say? Oh, yes. Now I know. You are very sensitive about your weight [your intelligence, your competence]. That's where I'll strike: "You're fat [stupid, incompetent].

There. You did it. You just succeeded in harming your partner, your relationship, and probably yourself. But it sure felt good for a minute.

You do have a choice, though. Let's play this scene again, but this time revise it a little.

a. I'm really mad at you.

b. I'm so mad that part of me desperately wants to say or do something that will make you feel awful.

c. I'm tempted, but should I?

d. No; as much as I want to insult you right now I'm not going to do it. That's not what love is about.

e. Instead, I'll get away for a few minutes until I can calm down or I'll say something caring and thoughtful to get past the anger.

Now, that act of nonaggression took courage, character, and control. It wasn't easy because you were so angry, your fight-or-flight instincts had been activated. Furthermore, most likely nobody will ever realize what you just chose not to do. But you will know.

Why make that choice not to attack? There are several good reasons. First, you'll probably feel good about yourself. You handled that situation as an adult, with dignity and self-control. Second, you'll avoid feeling guilty about harming someone you love. After all, people don't get into relationships just to have someone to bash around. Loving someone means helping him or her feel good, not bad. Third, your choosing not to go for the jugular makes it far less likely that your partner will go for yours. Finally, you'll never resolve any conflicts by attacking each other's character and personality. If you actually hope to settle that issue about finances or spending time with each other or sex, you must avoid saying things that guarantee your partner will become defensive.

Here's a short writing exercise to go with the ideas we've just written. *Please do not share the results of this exercise with your partner.* This one is for you and only you.

Write down four especially nasty things that you have said to your partner during the heat of battle.

1. _____

2. _____

3. _____

4. _____

Now check off the positive results you may have received from saying those things.

____ Immediate satisfaction          ____ A feeling of power

____ I got what I wanted             ____ A sense of superiority

____ A sense of victory              ____ Excitement/energy

____ Something else (What?_____)

And now check off the negative results from saying those things.

____ My partner said something equally nasty back.

____ I felt guilty or ashamed of myself.

____ I just got even more angry.

____ I could have lost (or did lose) the relationship.

____ I felt out of control.

____ I didn't get what I wanted.

____ It only made things worse.

____ My partner stayed distant from me for quite a while.

____ I felt really stupid.

____ Other (What? _____ )

And now complete this sentence: The next time I feel like saying something terribly hurtful to my partner, I will _____

_____

because _____ .

# PART TWO

# How to Show Love

# Show your love by making time for your partner

"I work sixty hours a week. I'm exhausted by the time I get home. And there they are, the kids, waiting for me, all three of them, demanding attention. So I play with them. Then supper. Then bedtime stories. And after all that my wife [husband, partner] says, 'You never spend time with me' and she's [he's] unhappy. What am I supposed to do?"

Let's face facts. Chances are your life is busy, busy, busy. You hustle from one task to another. You sleep less than you should. You eat fast food. You're constantly tired, but you have to keep going.

No wonder, then, that spending time with your partner gradually gets sacrificed. It's not usually a conscious choice so much as a slowly developing pattern. You go from taking hours each day alone with your partner to just scraping out a few minutes, and from doing things as a couple to only doing family activities. You talk less about important things. You joke around less with each other. Even your sex life erodes because you don't have time to feel very romantic. Worst of all, there seems to be no alternative. You feel stuck in this not very satisfying pattern because you have so much to do. You feel trapped.

There is a way out of this trap, however. It's called *reprioritizing*. That means going from a list that probably looks like this: #1, job; #2, kids; #3,

**SMART SAYING**

*Come out of the circle of time, and into the circle of love.*

—RUMI

85

chores: #4, other responsibilities; #5, partner to a new list that goes #1, partner; #2, everything else. Is that possible? Certainly! Is it easy? Actually, it's not as hard as you may think.

- *First, tell yourself that nothing, absolutely nothing, is more important to you than spending time alone with your partner.* That must be your first choice because otherwise everything else will squeeze it out.

- *Next, set a goal of spending at least thirty minutes a day alone with your partner.* We're not talking about a pie-in-the-sky, wouldn't-that-be-nice dream, either. This has to be a real goal that you fully intend to keep.

- *Figure out how you are going to make that happen.* The best way is to develop a routine so you don't have to plan each day. For example, "We'll put the kids to bed fifteen minutes earlier every night and then spend a half hour just talking with each other before we go to bed."

- *And then, make sure you follow through.* That might mean telling the kids they cannot interrupt your evening half hour for anything short of a calamity; it might mean turning off the phone; it might mean leaving some work behind so you can get home on time.

- *Finally, allow yourself no wiggle room.* That means not accepting any excuses or explanations about why you can't take that time with your partner. Simply said, taking time with your partner must be so important to you that you make it happen. If you accept one excuse today ("I'm sorry, honey, but just tonight I have to stay longer at work"), then there will be another excuse tomorrow ("The car needs an oil change") and another the next day ("Joey needs me to help him prepare for his spelling test").

Here is a place for you to devise your game plan. Needless to say, you should make this plan with your partner since it involves both of you. But you and only you must take responsibility for carving out the time from your schedule to be with your partner. And while we can make space here for you to write down a few details, only you can make spending time with your partner your highest priority in life.

*Making My Partner My Highest Priority Plan*

My goal is to spend at least thirty minutes a day alone with my partner.
Here's my plan.

The best time to do this is from _____ to _____

In order to make that happen, I will have to spend less time on _____

_____

_____

During that thirty minutes I will make sure we aren't interrupted by

_____

_____

The people I need to tell about my plan (so they won't expect me to
take that time away from my partner) are _____

_____

_____

I won't let myself use the following excuses to keep me from spending
time with my partner: _____

_____

_____

_____

The most important reason I have to stick with this plan is _____

_____

_____

_____

# The doubly loving relationship: Becoming helpmates and best friends

We believe that two traditions of marriage coexist in America (and probably in most countries). On the one hand, we want to work well with our partner: the old term "helpmeet" applies here, which we'll modify to "helpmate." In a well-functioning marriage, the partners are like two horses hitched to a heavy cart. Together, if they work harmoniously, they can pull that cart a long way. But we also want our partner to be our best friend: someone we can talk with about anything, play with, and generally enjoy. While the helpmate metaphor is two horses pulling a cart, the best friend model is more like two people holding hands walking side by side down the path of life.

Sometimes we meet couples in marriage counseling whose main problem is that one of them believes almost exclusively in the helpmate model while the other is totally tied to the best friend concept. The helpmate advocate thinks, "Life is hard. There's always a lot to get done. The house has to be painted. The kids need to be fed. I've got to have help with all this stuff or I'll fall apart." This person's chief complaint is that his or her partner doesn't do enough, doesn't carry a full load. The worst thing the helpmate person can call someone is "lazy." That shows how much he or she values working together. Meanwhile, the best friend advocate thinks,

"I didn't get into this relationship simply to work and work and work. I want romance, long talks, and closeness. I want my partner to tell me everything and I want to do the same." The best friend person's worst insult is that someone is "distant," which shows how much he or she values intimacy.

Before continuing, let's see how you feel about these two ideas.

First, rate the importance to you of each of the following two statements with a number between 0 and 10, with 0 meaning "No, that's not what I want at all" and 10 meaning "Absolutely, that's what I most want in life." Make sure you put down what you really want, not what you think you should put down. Ask yourself if your answers reflect the day-to-day decisions you make about your relationship.

SMART TIP

Give your partner two red roses, each with a note.

The first note says "For the one I love,"

And the second "For my best friend."

1. More than anything else I want my partner in life to be my helpmate. _____

2. More than anything else I want my partner in life to be my best friend. _____

If you are currently in a relationship, please also guess how your partner might score those same two sentences. _____   _____

Now would be a good time for you to discuss your answers with your partner if that is possible. Make sure that the goal of your talk is acceptance, not persuasion. You won't succeed in convincing your partner to change his or her values and beliefs about committed relationships, so don't try. But a good talk about your respective priorities might help you find ways for each of you to feel more loved and appreciated.

Partners in every relationship must negotiate the differences they have in this area. For example, chances are you will have difficulty at least from time to time if you rate the importance of your partner's being your best friend an 8 and a helpmate a 2 while your partner rates the importance of your being his or her best friend a 3 and his or her helpmate a 7. You mostly want someone you can work beside while your partner wants more of a soul mate. But remember this: *being someone's helpmate or best friend are both ways of showing love.* Neither way is always better than the other.

You and your partner don't have to choose between these two ways of showing love because a loving relationship thrives on both elements. Yes, it certainly is important to pull that cart together. You get more done that way. And yes, by all means let's become best friends while we're pulling that cart. Let's even remember to unhitch it often enough to have lots of fun together. Taking turns being helpmates and best friends can make your relationship glow with love.

Besides, there is plenty of room to be both helpmates and best friends at the same time. Imagine, for instance, constructing a retaining wall together while discussing that powerful movie you watched last night. Or jointly putting in a flower bed you don't absolutely need but that will make your home a little nicer. Why settle for one or the other when sometimes, if you look for opportunities, you can have both?

See if you can answer the following questions.

Can you note three times within the last month that you and your partner have been helpmates to each other)?

1. _____

2. _____

3. _____

Can you note three times in the last month you and your partner have been best friends to each other?

1. _____

2. _____

3. _____

Can you note three times in the last month that you and your partner have done something during which you felt like both helpmates and best friends to each other?

1. _____

2. _____

3. _____

What kind of helpmate activities could you do together?

1. _____

2. _____

3. _____

What kind of best friend activities could you do together?

1. _____

2. _____

3. _____

What kind of mutual helpmate and best friend activities could you do together?

1. _____

2. _____

3. _____

# Listen with love

"You know when I most feel loved? It's when my partner stops everything, sits down, and really listens to me. That's when I feel truly important to him [her]."

How true is the statement above for you? For your partner? One of the strongest complaints people make in marriage counseling is that their partner doesn't listen to them. They don't usually mean that the other person completely ignores them, though. What they mean is that they don't get the sense that their partner is paying loving attention to them. They need their partner to listen with his or her ears, mind, and heart. When that doesn't happen, they feel distant from their partner. But when they do sense that their partner is listening that way, they feel deeply cherished. Simply stated, one of the best ways to show your partner your caring is to listen with love.

Listening with love takes concentration, energy, and a willingness to put your own thoughts on the back burner for a while.

Here are some suggestions for listening with love.

1. *Issue an invitation to your partner* to talk so you can listen with love.
   Listening with love is a skill. You will get better at it the more you practice. So how do you get opportunities to practice? By asking your partner at least once a day to talk about things that matter to him or her and then making it your goal to listen with love.

SMART SAYING

O Great Spirit

Help me always

To speak the truth
   quietly

To listen with an
   open mind

When others speak

And to remember
   the peace

That may be found
   in silence.

—CHEROKEE PRAYER

2. *Put aside any distractions* that might keep you from listening.

Turn off the TV. Tell the kids to go play by themselves for awhile. Just as important, set aside any thoughts or concerns that might distract you from paying full attention to your partner. Remind yourself that you would want your partner to fully attend to you if you had something important on your mind.

3. *Take a positive attitude* when your partner begins speaking.

Don't get defensive. Don't be judgmental. You can't both listen with love and criticize your partner. Instead, tell yourself that your partner is an intelligent, thoughtful person whose ideas are worth listening to.

4. *Let your partner know you are listening nonverbally* through eye contact, touch, nods, and facial expressions.

Listening with love is a full-body activity. You need to look right at your partner (with loving, not glaring, eyes). Occasional gentle touches convey the message "I'm here with you; keep talking" without distracting your partner. Nods say "Yes, I hear you" as well as "I agree with you." Facial expressions are especially important if you have a tendency to listen with a blank look. Your partner may read a blank expression to mean "I'm not really interested in what you're saying," so make sure you let your face show some reaction to your partner's words.

5. *Keep the focus on your partner* rather than talking about yourself.

Listening with love is not a typical back-and-forth conversation. Normally, one person talks for a while about himself or herself and then the other takes over. But in listening with love you need to keep the focus on your partner. Your job is to draw out your partner, to keep him or her talking. So don't switch the topic to yourself. Above all, don't take over the conversation so that your partner thinks, "Hey, I started to tell _____ about myself, and now all we're doing is talking about him [her]."

6. *Ask questions* that encourage your partner to keep sharing his or her thoughts and feelings.

"What do you think about that?" "What's most important to you about what you just said?" "Would you tell me more about that?" "How could you make that happen?" "What do you want?" "What kind of help do you need from me?"

Note: Be careful about asking "why questions" as in, "Why are you doing that?" Why questions often feel like judgments or accusations rather than simple requests for information.

7. *Listen for emotions* by homing in on feeling words.

There's one more loving question you can ask: "What are you feeling?" That's an invitation for your partner to share emotions: sadness, joy, loneliness, hurt, anger, shame, guilt, love, emptiness, fear, grief, pain, distress, pride, and so on. Most people feel loved when their partner gives them encouragement both to have and express feelings. That's when they sense that their partner will go with them into the scary parts of life.

8. *Let yourself respond emotionally* to your partner's message.

It's important to listen with your mind. It's even more important to listen with your heart. That means allowing yourself to feel some of your partner's pain and joy. It means noticing your emotional responses to your partner's words and feelings. Now, you don't want to get so distracted by your emotional responses that you quit paying attention to your partner. But you do want to get at least a little emotional.

9. *Read between the lines.*

Notice what your partner doesn't say as well as what he or she does say. People don't always say everything they could or exactly what they're thinking. Sometimes they hint. They may choose to use gentle words designed not to hurt their partner's feelings instead of really saying what's on their mind. They may share their thoughts but not their feelings. Perhaps they stop what they're saying, pause, and then switch to another topic. You will notice these things if you ask yourself, "What is my partner leaving out or not quite saying right now?" Be careful not to make any assumptions, though. Remember that your partner is the expert here, not you. However, pointing out hesitations, topic switches, lack of feeling words, or similar omissions may be very helpful to your partner as he or she attempts to communicate with you.

10. *Save your suggestions* until they are requested.

   Some people, especially men, are so eager to help their partners solve problems that they rush ahead with ideas, suggestions, and plans. The problem is that their partners mostly want them to listen rather than advise. So save your ideas on what to do until your partner asks for them. Then remember that your suggestions are just that—suggestions. Don't take offense if your partner doesn't follow them.

11. *Be willing to be influenced* by your partner's ideas and concerns.

   John Gottman stresses that good listeners do more than listen to their partner's thoughts, ideas, concerns, and suggestions. They also think about those ideas and change what they say or do in response. For instance, a woman says to her husband, "John, you're working too hard. I want you to take some time off." Notice the difference between responding "Yeah, yeah, she always says that" and "You know, she's right. I'll see about taking next Friday off." Now, of course people don't always accept their partner's suggestions. The point is to take them seriously all the time and act on them at least occasionally.

## Summary of How to Listen with Love

1. *Issue an invitation* to your partner to talk so you can listen with love.

2. *Put aside any distractions* that might keep you from listening.

3. *Take a positive attitude* when your partner begins speaking.

4. *Let your partner know you are listening nonverbally* through eye contact, touch, nods, and facial expressions.

5. *Keep the focus on your partner* rather than talking about yourself.

6. *Ask questions* that encourage your partner to keep sharing his or her thoughts and feelings.

7. *Listen for emotions* by homing in on feeling words.

8. *Let yourself respond emotionally* to your partner's message.

9. *Read between the lines.*

10. *Save your suggestions* until they are requested.

11. *Be willing to be influenced* by your partner's ideas and concerns.

Which three of the listening with love suggestions have been most difficult for you?

_____

_____

_____

These are the ones you need to begin changing so you can listen better. Set yourself the goal of improving these areas first by really focusing on them when you are having a conversation with your partner. Then, when you have a chance to think about that conversation, ask yourself how you did in each area. Also, if possible, get feedback from your partner. For example, if you picked numbers 3, 5, and 7, ask your partner how you've done on staying positive, keeping the focus on your partner, and asking questions and listening for feelings. Just make sure you listen with love to that feedback. It would be pretty silly, wouldn't it, to get defensive about whether you were getting defensive?

Some of you might want to give yourself a score for each time you try to listen with love to your partner. Here's how: There are eleven suggestions above. Rate each one from 0 to 4.

0: You didn't do that at all during the conversation

1: You thought about doing that but didn't

2: You tried to do that but don't think you succeeded

3: You did that once while you were listening

4: You did that more than once while you were listening

You could score from 0 to 44 points per conversation. Your goal should be to keep improving your score in general and/or to improve one or two specific areas each time you try to listen with love.

First Attempt

1) _____    2) _____    3) _____    4) _____    5) _____
6) _____    7) _____    8) _____    9) _____    10) _____
11) _____    Total _____

Second Attempt

1) _____    2) _____    3) _____    4) _____    5) _____
6) _____    7) _____    8) _____    9) _____    10) _____
11) _____    Total _____

Third Attempt

1) _____    2) _____    3) _____    4) _____    5) _____
6) _____    7) _____    8) _____    9) _____    10) _____
11) _____    Total _____

# Show love by understanding your partner

Feeling alone. Separate. Distant. *Misunderstood.*

Feeling connected. Close. *Deeply understood.*

Both of these states are possible in a relationship. But almost everyone prefers the latter. Indeed, the main purpose of this book is to help people become more connected, close, and deeply understood.

This exercise specifically deals with learning how to better understand your partner. That's because taking the time and effort to understand your partner is one of the best ways to demonstrate love. Just think of how wonderful you felt the last time someone really understood what you were saying—not just the words but also your feelings, values, and dreams.

Here's an example of what we're talking about. Melody, a thirty-five-year-old medical secretary, is talking with her husband, Terry, about the future. These are her words: "Terry, I'm a little tired of my job." But this is what she means: "Terry, I'm so sick of my job I could die. I'm bored out of my mind. I can feel myself getting more depressed every day. I want to quit, but I'm afraid you'll think I'm being irresponsible. I don't know what to do." Now, Terry isn't a mind reader. He can't be expected always to hear what Melody isn't saying. But notice the difference between these possible responses.

SMART STRATEGY

Everybody has a best time of day to listen. It might be early morning, late afternoon, or just before bedtime. So if you really want to understand your partner better, ask him or her to talk with you at the time you are at your best.

- A nonresponse: "Say, did you know the Packers are on TV tonight?"

- A critical response: "Well, you can't quit now. We need the money."

- A quick-solution response: "Okay, just quit your job if you don't like it."

- *An understanding response*: "That sounds serious. And you're looking sad. What's the problem?"

The understanding response is different from the others in several ways. First, Terry recognizes that Melody just said something important. Second, he notices her emotion. Third, he invites her to say more. It's likely, with that kind of encouragement, that Melody will gradually be able to speak her thoughts, hopes, and fears. She will also probably come up with her own solution to this problem. Certainly she will feel loved. And that's our main point. One of the best ways you can show your partner your love is by taking the time and energy to understand him or her.

There is one word that is highly associated with deep understanding: *empathy*. Here are some useful definitions of empathy.

1. "The bridge spanning the chasm that separates us from each other." —Arthur Ciaramicoli

2. "Active, searching, reaching out toward the other."—John Berecz

3. "The capacity to understand and respond to the unique experiences of another."—Arthur Ciaramicoli

4. "Understanding each person's interest and viewpoint."—Terry Hargrave

5. "Emotionally understanding the other."—John Berecz

Each of these definitions says something a little different about empathy. The first hints at why empathy is such an important way to show love. Empathy is a way to get outside of yourself. It helps each of us meet on that bridge that connects "me" with "you." That leads to the second definition. Each of us can become more empathic only by actively walking out onto that bridge. We must reach out to our partner. As we do that we will gradually learn how to better understand and respond to him or her. It's particularly important, as the author and psychologist Arthur Ciaramicoli states in the third definition, to realize that your partner has had many unique experiences that have shaped his or her life. Some of these experiences may have been terrible (being sexually abused as a child); others may have been wonderful (having been taught to trust the universe by a generous and loving father). Some may be permanent (being an only child) and others short-lived (suffering a broken collarbone in a traffic accident). But every significant experience has affected your partner's thoughts, feelings, and worldview. Your partner will feel deeply understood, and loved, if you can begin to see the world that he or she experiences.

The fourth and fifth definitions of empathy are more specific about how empathy works.

Terry Hargrave, a marriage counselor and author of several books on forgiveness, writes that empathy involves "understanding each person's interest and viewpoint." He's stressing the need to find out what your partner thinks about important things in your lives. Another thoughtful author, John Berecz, adds that empathy also involves "emotionally understanding the other." His emphasis is on your partner's feelings.

Very well, you may be thinking about now, that sounds like good theory. But exactly *how* can I get on that bridge? What do I have to do? Well, mostly what you need to do is fairly simple: *ask lots of questions* and then *really listen without criticism* to your partner's answers.

Here's an exercise to help you deeply understand your partner.

Think of two things about your partner's childhood that may have strongly affected him or her. Make one of them something bad or unfortunate that happened (losing a parent, parental divorce, moving around a lot, physical abuse, etc.), the other something good or fortunate (having loving grandparents, growing up financially secure, having wonderful holiday traditions, etc.). Don't pick something you've already talked about over the years. Instead, select two of your partner's early experiences that you really would like to learn more about.

Please write those two experiences down here.

1. _____

2. _____

Now ask your partner to set aside about an hour so you can ask him or her some questions about these experiences. Pick a time and place where you won't get interrupted. Then begin the conversation something like this: "_____, I want to learn more about you so I can understand you better. So let me ask you a few questions about things that happened in your childhood. I'd like to learn how you were affected by those experiences."

Here are several questions that will help your partner respond.

- What do you remember about that time in your life?

- Do you remember any details about what happened that day or during that time?

- How was what happened good? Bad? Happy? Sad?

- What emotions did you feel at that time?

- What feelings do you have right now as you're telling me about that time in your life?

- What long-term effects did that experience have on you? How did it affect your way of seeing the world as you were growing up? How is it still affecting you?

- What lessons did you learn from that experience?

- What do you want most for me to remember about what you've been telling me?

- Is there anything else you want to tell me about that experience before I ask you about one more?

As you listen, remember, (1) the goal is to understand your partner, not to change or advise him or her; (2) listen for feelings as well as words; (3) listen with your heart as well as your mind; and (4) don't switch the conversation to yourself even if something your partner says reminds you of your own experiences.

Here's an example. Pammy has mentioned once or twice that she had a wonderful Christmas when she was twelve years old even though her grandmother was dying and barely able to talk. Pammy's partner, Hardy, decides to ask her about that time in her life. He asks all the questions we suggested. Here are brief versions of Pammy's answers.

Q: What do you remember about that time in your life?

A: I was confused. I understood the idea of death but had never experienced it. I didn't know how to treat Grandma—whether to try to talk with her or run away.

Q: Do you remember any details about what happened that day or during that time?

A: I remember the star on top of the Christmas tree. It was bright white. And I remember how shriveled Grandma's hands were when she reached out to me.

Q: How was what happened good? Bad? Happy? Sad?

A: It was good because it was my last chance to be with my grandma. It was bad because I knew I'd never have another Christmas with her. I was happy when Grandma gave me her special brooch—the silver one I still keep in my jewelry box. And of course I was very sad for Grandma.

Q: What emotions did you feel at that time?

A: Happy, sad, a little scared. Confused. Now that we're talking about it I remember that I even felt some anger toward Grandma. You know, how could she do this terrible thing—dying—to me? And guilty, because I was too afraid of Grandma right then to tell her how much I loved her. And then she died and I never got that last chance to tell her how important she was.

Q: What feelings do you have right now as you're telling me about that time in your life?

A: I'm feeling a little lonely. I still miss her so much. But I'm glad we're talking about her. It's almost like she's in this room with us.

Q: What long-term effects did that experience have on you? How did it affect your way of seeing the world as you were growing up? How is it still affecting you?

A: I think about death a lot. And sometimes I'm afraid you'll get sick and die and leave me just like Grandma did. Maybe that's why I'm always asking you to be extra careful.

Q: What lessons did you learn from that experience?

A: That was the first time I realized that people don't hang around forever. I made a vow after Grandma died to tell people I love them because if I wait too long I may never get to say it.

Q: What do you want most for me to remember about what you've been telling me?

A: I guess that I'm still scared and confused about death. I still don't know whether to get close or stay away when people get sick.

Q: Is there anything else you want to tell me about that experience?

A: Not now but maybe later now that you've got me thinking abut it.


Empathic questioning isn't only for childhood experiences. You can use this approach whenever you want to better understand your partner. Select a few more things to ask about, perhaps one from the more recent past and at least one involving something going on right now. Write those selections below.

_____

_____

_____


Empathy is a skill. It gets better the more you practice it. So keep questioning, listening to, and understanding your partner.

# Show love by accepting difference

"Yes, of course I love my partner. But if she made a couple of small changes, I'd like her more."

"He spends Tuesday nights with his buddies. I wish he'd stay home with me."

"She's more religious than I am. That makes me nervous."

Who doesn't want his or her partner to change some of his or her habits, interests, priorities, friends, or attitudes? Maybe all you want are a few changes here and there. Perhaps you want some big changes. How about both large and small changes? Almost everybody wants to make adjustments to his or her partner.

What do you think would happen if you could wave a magic wand and make your partner change in every way you desire? Our guess is that with each change, your partner would become more and more like you. For example, first you'd get rid of your partner's fondness for reading and substitute watching movies—which is what you like to do most with your spare time. Then out would go that mousy, quiet way of speaking for a more assertive approach—like yours. Then you'd dump that silly love of animals for a more realistic attitude, namely yours. And then . . . We think that you would eventually create a clone, your very own twin who acts,

SMART THOUGHT

Many people have a secret thought: "If only my partner was just like me everything would be great." Wrong! It's the differences between two people that make life interesting.

thinks, and sounds almost exactly like you. But is that really what you want from a partner?

What about difference? Think about what you gain from the fact that your partner has a somewhat different approach to life than you do:

Opportunities to try new things that you would never even think about doing.

A chance to learn about another way of experiencing the world.

Help solving problems from someone who approaches them differently than you would.

Challenges to your values and beliefs that help you decide what is important to you.

A little tension that keeps your relationship from growing stale.

*One of the best ways to demonstrate your love for your partner is to accept once and for all that he or she has a right to be different from you.*

*Acceptance* is the key word in the above sentence. It helps to break it down into three components: Acceptance means *tolerating, appreciating,* and *encouraging* your partner's differences. Think of these concepts as three steps on a ladder that leads to fully accepting your partner.

*Tolerating* your partner's difference is the first step toward full acceptance. You tolerate difference when even though you don't like what your partner is doing you don't try to stop him or her from doing it. Tolerance is important in handling all those small, annoying things your partner does differently from you (speaks fast, listens to country instead of rock music, skips breakfast, etc.). These are "take a deep breath and forget about it" issues, simply not worth fighting about. On the other hand, tolerance is also vital around big, relationship-threatening differences (for instance, if one person drinks regularly and the other hates what alcohol does to people). These kinds of differences will have to be negotiated carefully but are seldom resolved merely by insisting that the other person completely accept your values and beliefs.

The message that goes with tolerance is "I can handle the differences between us without making a huge fuss."

Please list some things your partner says, does, or believes that you could learn to tolerate better.

_____

_____

_____

*Appreciating* difference takes you up another step on the ladder toward accepting your partner. Now you realize that the way your partner approaches life works pretty well. You love your partner now not only because of your similarities but also because of your differences. And you're willing to learn from your partner, maybe even to try out some of the ways he or she acts, thinks, and feels. For example, instead of grimacing when your partner begins talking about different religious views, you ask questions about those views and then consider them.

The message that accompanies appreciating is "I like the differences between us, and I want you to be the person you are."

In what areas could you be more appreciative of your partner?

_____

_____

_____

The third step up the ladder of acceptance is *encouraging* difference. Now you actively embrace difference instead of fearing it. For instance, you may have no interest in hiking but you help your partner find time to hike and you listen with interest to stories about hiking. You do this simply because you recognize that hiking makes your partner feel good.

The message in encouraging your partner is "I want you to have the best life possible so I'll help you do what is important to you even though it is different from what I would do."

What could you say or do that would encourage your partner to do things that are different from what you do?

_____

_____

_____

Remember, one of the best ways to demonstrate your love for your partner is to accept once and for all that he or she has a right to be different from you.

# Love needs trust to form a strong bond

"I love you. You can trust me."

It isn't always easy to trust another human being. Trust involves vulnerability, and being vulnerable means you could get hurt.

Just because you love your partner or your partner loves you doesn't necessarily mean that you trust each other. It's certainly possible to love without trust. But usually relationships based only on love, those in which trust is absent, are unstable. They break down easily in the midst of lies, omissions, and irresponsibility. However, coupling love with trust is like supergluing two people together. The bond created when love is mixed with trust becomes almost unbreakable. One difference between love and superglue, though, is that developing trust is a slow process, made even slower if your partner has been betrayed in the past. That's why it's so important for you to be consistently trustworthy.

We wrote in the introduction that just saying "I love you" is not enough. You must show your love as well if you want your partner to feel loved. That idea goes double in matters of trust. You can't expect your partner to trust you unless you act in a trustworthy manner.

What does it mean to be trustworthy? Here are five traits of a trustworthy person.

**SMART HUMOR**

When you make a
    promise,

Don't be an
    ignoramus

Just to keep it

And repeat it

Does away with
    Doubting Thomas

—PATRICIA
POTTER-EFRON

1. He or she says the truth, especially in important conversations with his or her partner.

2. He or she doesn't omit important things from conversations, even when mentioning them might be embarrassing or troubling.

3. He or she keeps promises, not only big ones (like a vow to be sexually faithful) but also little day-to-day agreements.

4. He or she behaves responsibly, reliably, and consistently, demonstrating in daily routines that he or she can be depended on.

5. He or she admits when he or she has screwed up and makes amends.

The challenge is to do all five of these things all of the time. Perhaps, being merely human, that is asking too much. We all fail the test of trustworthiness once in a while. But *if you want to build trust in your relationship, your goal should be to be completely trustworthy*, not to be mostly trustworthy or trustworthy when it's convenient. One warning: although being honest is an important part of building trust, remember that you can be tactful and honest at the same time. You won't build trust through honesty if you pair honesty with cruelty, tactlessness, crudeness, or thoughtlessness.

How trustworthy are you? Next to each of the following statements, place a 0 for "almost never," a 1 for "sometimes," a 2 for "often," a 3 for "most of the time," or a 4 for "always."

1. I tell my partner the truth, especially in important conversations. _____

2. I don't omit important things from conversations even when mentioning them might be embarrassing or troubling. _____

3. I keep promises, not only big ones but also little day-to-day agreements. _____

4. I behave responsibly, reliably, and consistently, demonstrating in daily routines that my partner can depend on me. _____

5. I admit when I have screwed up and make amends. _____

What's your total score? Is it at least 15 points, meaning that you are averaging 3 points an item? If not, you've probably got a lot of work to do.

Where do you most need to change so you can become more trustworthy? We suggest that you pick the one item of these five that would help the most and then start working on it right away. Remember one thing as you do so, though: you don't increase your trustworthiness by making promises. You only become more trustworthy by keeping them.

# Show your love by respecting your partner

Understanding the word *respect* is absolutely critical if two people want to have a mutually loving relationship. That's because relationships without respect quickly become ugly and nasty as each partner says things that are particularly hurtful to the other. Being in a relationship without respect is like sitting in a rowboat heading over Niagara Falls. Worse yet, it's like being the two people sitting in that boat who refuse to pick up their oars because they're too busy shouting insults at each other.

So what does it mean to respect someone? Perhaps the single most helpful definition of respect we've discovered is this one: "to show regard and consideration" (*Random House Unabridged Dictionary*, Second Edition). In addition to being generally polite and thoughtful, showing regard and consideration includes listening carefully to your partner and respecting his or her privacy.

The flip side of respect is called, naturally enough, disrespect. Disrespectful behavior is usually shaming in that one person says or implies that there is something wrong with the other. Basically the shamer says that the other person is stupid, bad, or worthless. The shamer is a judge who constantly convicts people of being no good, not good enough, or unlovable. But what exactly does it mean to show regard and consideration to your partner? Here is a quick Dos and Don'ts list.

## If You Want to Show Respect to Your Partner, Do

- Begin each day with a commitment to treat your partner with respect.

- Remember to be as polite to your partner as you would be to a guest in your home.

- Look for and comment on the good things your partner says and does.

- Let your partner know that you appreciate his or her basic personality.

- Listen carefully and attentively to what your partner says to you.

- Support your partner's wants, needs, hopes, and dreams.

- Tell others what you appreciate about your partner in his or her presence.

- Regularly accept your partner's choices without trying to change him or her.

- Treat your partner as your equal in every way.

- Substitute praise for criticism.

- Laugh at yourself, not at your partner.

- Affirm your partner's rights to privacy, personal time, and a life of his or her own.

**SMART DEFINITION**

In Latin, *specto* means "to look at." Thus, to respect someone is to look at them . . . again.

## If You Want to Show Respect to Your Partner, Don't

- Constantly criticize your partner.

- Swear at your partner.

- Say or imply that your partner is bad, evil, stupid, worthless, incompetent, or ugly.

- Say nasty things to your partner in front of others.

- Ignore what your partner is saying or act as if he or she isn't there.

- Act superior to your partner.

- Tell your partner that he or she is unlovable.

- Act disgusted or greatly disappointed with your partner.

- Find things wrong with the way your partner says and does things.

- Tell your partner that he or she is not as good as someone else (make a negative comparison).

- Hit, push, shove, or physically threaten your partner.

- Regularly threaten to kick your partner out of your life and find someone better.

- Try to control everything your partner does (to run that person's life).

- Refuse to say "I love you" just because you are angry with him or her.

Please take a good, long look at these two lists. Circle the items on the Dos list that you most need to remember. These are the things that you want to do more often. They will increase your respect toward your partner. Then circle the items on the Don'ts list that you most need to work on. These are the things you have been doing that decrease the amount of respect you show your partner.

The next step is to decide which one or two items on each list you will focus on changing. Select no more than two items from each list so you aren't overwhelmed. Then take the next week to practice them. For example, if you select "Don't find things wrong with the way your partner says and does things" and "Do remember to be as polite to your partner as you would be to a guest in your home," think about those two items every day. Make sure you refrain from excessive negativity and at the same time remember to ask for things politely and to say thank you even for small acts of kindness your partner shows you. Be a little tough on yourself here. Don't make excuses for acts of disrespect or for failing to show respect when you could have. Your goal should be to show respect to your partner the entire day.

One important note: please don't turn these lists into a "See, honey, this is what you are doing wrong" lecture. That's not respectful. Instead, keep the focus on what you need to do in order to demonstrate that you respect your partner. Make the changes you need to make. Keep making them. Chances are pretty good that if you do, your partner will get the idea and treat you more respectfully, too.

# There's a difference between having sex and making love

Your use of language may differ from ours. But for us, "having sex" denotes the physical act of intercourse. "Making love" includes having sex but adds the verbal, emotional, and spiritual connections that take place during sexual union. Of the two experiences only making love creates true intimacy. As wonderful as it is to have sex with each other, making love is even better.

We defined intimacy before as "two people sharing their private worlds with each other and deeply respecting each other's disclosures." We added that a couple achieves intimacy when each takes the risk of sharing secrets and both respond with loving, caring, interest, and acceptance. Intimacy begins when one person decides, "I'll take a chance by telling you something important about myself" and the other responds, "Go ahead. We're in this together. You can trust me with whatever you tell me. And I'll tell you about myself, too."

There is nothing about having sex that automatically makes it more than a way to achieve physical pleasure. Two people can remain basically hidden from each other even while they take care of their needs. They can even become sexual athletes, having sex with great skill but no emotion, the equivalent of overly practiced ballroom dancers who perfect every step while looking at each other with frozen smiles. These sexual athletes often

**SMART SAYING**

*Love is often the fruit of marriage.*
—FRENCH SAYING

117

seem willing to sacrifice emotional connection in their quest for the perfect orgasm.

Now, there's nothing wrong with pure and simple pleasure. We're not suggesting that every time a couple hits the sack they must achieve the heights of intimacy. Sometimes—many times—the goal of having sex is physical release. But not always. Sometimes people want more than that. They want to feel deeply connected not only physically but also emotionally and spiritually. They want this particular act of intercourse to become an intimate experience.

And what better place than the bedroom could there be to discover real intimacy? Sexual intercourse is by its very nature an intensely private event. We close the door. We speak in whispers. We say and do things that we would not want people to watch or overhear. We let ourselves be vulnerable to each other. We let go of control. What an opportunity to experience every aspect of mutual connection.

There is no single formula to turn having sex into making love. Each couple does that in their own way. However, we can offer some suggestions that might help you move in that direction.

- *Don't rush.* Hurried sex is never intimate sex. Take your time getting started, while you're at it, and afterward.

- *Seduce your partner's heart as well as his or her body.* Say and do what you've learned really makes your partner feel loved during intercourse. If you don't know, ask.

- *Take some risks.* Share a fantasy. Try something different. Risk feeling silly or foolish. Risk rejection for the sake of possible acceptance.

- *Encourage your partner to tell you what he or she really wants.* It's okay to say no to those desires, of course, but consider saying yes in the spirit of mutual adventure.

- *Think of sexuality as adult playtime.* Have fun. Laugh. Enjoy.

- *Take great joy in helping your partner feel wonderful.* Gently invite your partner to abandon control.

- *Accept what is offered.* Start with the idea that your partner owes you nothing in the area of sexuality. Graciously accept what you receive without expecting or demanding more.

- *Remember to say thank you.*

- *Relax.* Don't let an opportunity for intimacy be spoiled by focusing on performance. In particular, don't fret about getting to orgasm or getting your partner there. You'll get there when you get there. And sometimes sexual union can be satisfying without orgasm.

- *Show appreciation for and refrain from criticizing your partner* (or yourself) before, during, or after intercourse. The kind of intimacy we're discussing only takes place in an atmosphere of trust, safety, and acceptance. In particular, make only positive comments about your partner's body.

- *Focus your mind on the present.* Intimacy happens when your mind is completely focused on the moment. Place your distractions on a mental shelf while you make love. They'll be right there waiting for you when you're done.

We suggest you read this list over the next time you start thinking about making love. Select one or two ideas from the list that you will remember. Use them. Enjoy.

# One of the best times to show your love is during conflict

"Honey, I don't agree with you at all. I think you're wrong and I'm right. But I still love you a lot."

One of the best times to show that you love your partner is during a conflict. Why? Because most people fall away from secure attachment during fights with their partners and become more fearful, preoccupied, or dismissive. They may look and sound angry, but they probably feel insecure, highly emotional, and disconnected. In other words, it's just plain hard to feel loved during an argument. So that's exactly when people most need to get some reassurance. They need to hear right then and there that they are loved. Telling your partner about your love reassures him or her that your love is strong enough to weather any disagreement, however serious or long lasting. It is one of the strongest statements of faith you can make.

So the first thing to remember is to say "I love you" to your partner even during conflict. But there are other ways to show your partner your love during a disagreement. There are also some unloving things you will want to avoid doing. Let's begin with those by reviewing some of the work of John Gottman.

Dr. Gottman, who wrote *The Seven Principles for Making Marriage Work*, has researched couples for years. His goal is to be able to predict which couples will eventually divorce and which will stay married. He's discovered many strong predictors of divorce. Four of them are being excessively critical of one's partner, expressing contempt, being too defensive, and "stonewalling" (refusing to discuss issues). These are negative behaviors that certainly must be avoided in any deeply loving relationship. It's particularly important to avoid them during conflicts. Just think about how any of those behaviors almost guarantees that a small conflict will quickly escalate into a major dispute. Criticism, contempt, defensiveness, and stonewalling create distance and diminish love.

Now let's talk about what helps keep the heat down during a conflict. Again, John Gottman's research is very helpful.

Dr. Gottman documented that, probably to nobody's surprise, just about every couple disagrees, argues, and fights. No two people can agree about everything over the years. Some conflict is absolutely normal. Furthermore, the sheer amount of conflict did *not* predict divorce. Some stable couples disagreed a lot, others infrequently. What did matter, though, was *how* they argued. Gottman discovered that what really helped was when the women in long-term relationships "softened" the start of a possible conflict discussion ("Honey, I really appreciate your feeding the baby, but she was supposed to get bananas, not ground chuck" versus "How could you feed the baby ground chuck! Use your head!") and when men reacted less defensively ("Okay, I'll listen to what she's saying" versus "How dare you criticize me!") and let their partners influence their thoughts and actions ("Hmm, maybe she has a point there" versus "She's an idiot. I'm right and that's all there's to it"). Gottman's findings seem to stress the need for couples to be civil during disagreements. This is your partner, after all, not the enemy.

Here's a list of some other things, in addition to "I love you," that you can say and do during a conflict that will help your partner feel loved.

- Offer to get your partner a soft drink, a cup of coffee, or a snack.

- Give or accept a hug (but only if your partner agrees; ask first).

- Say positive things about your partner's ideas instead of criticizing ("You know, what you just said does make sense even though I still can't agree with your main point").

- Stay calm: breathe deeply, talk slowly, sit down, keep your voice soft.

- Fight fair: be polite, stay on topic, don't swear, don't attack your partner's personality.

- Look for mutually agreeable solutions to your disagreements. Be willing to negotiate and compromise.

- Be respectful: avoid shaming, humiliating, and blaming statements. These are not ways to demonstrate your love. In fact, they undermine love every time you use them. If you do say something rude or thoughtless, apologize immediately and don't do it again.

- Be forgiving and accepting. Your partner can't say and do everything exactly the way you'd like, especially during a disagreement. So don't take things too personally. Don't get oversensitive. Cut your partner a little slack, and with any luck he or she will do the same for you.

- Try to end your disagreement with an act of reconnection. A hug or a kiss can be very reassuring at the end of an argument. It's a way to say the fight is over and your love is strong. But again, only hug or kiss if your partner agrees. Some people simply have to get away for a while before they can reconnect comfortably.

Think back to the last time you had a disagreement with your partner. Do you remember what you disagreed about?

_____

_____

Can you honestly say that you acted reassuringly to your partner during that conflict?  ____ Yes  ____ No

Why? _____

_____

Specifically, did you remember to say "I love you" during your argument?  ____ Yes  ____ No

How about at the end of the conflict. Did you suggest or accept a hug or a kiss?    ___ Yes    ___ No

And afterward? How quickly were you able to let go of your anger, fear, or hurt? Did it take:    ___ A few minutes    ___ A couple of hours ___ A day    ___ Longer than that    ___ I'm still upset

What did you do after the disagreement to heal the wounds to the relationship?

___ I told my partner I loved him or her.

___ I said something else positive to my partner. What was it?

_____

_____

___ I did something caring or thoughtful that showed my caring. What was it? _____

_____

___ Unfortunately I didn't do anything at all that I can remember.

Do you need to practice saying "I love you" during conflict? If so, ask your partner to do this exercise with you. It's an exaggeration exercise, so think of this as play.

- Select a topic to disagree about, preferably something not too heavy or touchy and not something one-sided (for example, something like whether to give your child sweet or nonsweet snacks is better than whether to have a child).

- Begin by your saying exactly one sentence about what you want. Then immediately add "and I love you."

- Your partner says one sentence and adds "I love you."

- Now you can take up to thirty seconds to speak your piece. However, you must say "I love you" at least once during those thirty seconds.

- Now your partner gets thirty seconds. The same rules apply.

- Now you can take up to one minute to make your case. Again, you must say "I love you" at least once.

- Your partner gets one minute. The same rules apply.

- You end by both telling each other, "I love you even when I don't agree with you."

- Stop. Discuss how that felt. Do it again if needed, switching to a new topic.

# Give your partner the gifts
# he or she really wants

It's five-year-old Joey's birthday party and finally he gets to unwrap that large present he's been eyeing for the last week. Joey eagerly rips open the package—and then bursts into tears. What happened? Well, Joey had convinced himself that the package contained a two-wheeler bike and instead it held a personal computer designed just for children.

Joey's parents feel really bad now. They were certain he would love that computer (even though Joey had asked for the two-wheeler on several occasions and never mentioned a computer). Dad was particularly disappointed because he loves computers himself and wouldn't mind at all receiving one as a present on his birthday. Now he's getting angry with his son for not liking the gift and at himself for making the wrong choice. Meanwhile, Mom is wondering if they should return the computer or insist that Joey learn to use it.

There's a little Joey inside every one of us when it comes to feeling loved. That's the part of us that knows exactly what we want from others. When we receive the right gift, we feel wonderful. But we feel bad when we are offered the wrong gift. Indeed, the Joey inside each of us may even feel unloved when we receive the wrong gift, thinking something like, "Sure, it's nice that she appreciates my looks, but what I want most is to be appreciated for how I think. I wish just once she'd say I made an intelligent remark."

> **SMART SAYING**
>
> *A gift consists not in what is done or given, but in the intention of the giver or the doer.*
> —SENECA

The problem here is not that this adult Joey's partner is being critical. No, she's actually trying to say something nice. She wants him to feel good. It's not her fault, but she's made the same mistake that little Joey's parents made. She's given him the wrong gift and now both of them feel unhappy and unappreciated.

**SMART TIP**

If your partner is a rock hound, bring a rock home or take him rock picking. If your partner likes tear-jerker novels, find them for her. Above all, if your partner feels loved when you're there, take a minute to really *be* there.

There must be a thousand ways you could show your love to your partner. But which of those thousand possibilities would make your partner feel most loved? How can you tell? It would be great if your partner always told you exactly what he or she wanted, but you can't count on that to happen every time (apparently the adult Joey in the example above hasn't yet told his partner about his need to be praised for his ideas). But certainly the first way to meet your partner's wants and needs is to listen carefully when he or she does express his or her desires or speaks in general about what makes him or her feel good. Another way is to notice whatever makes your partner's eyes light up with delight. A third way, naturally, is to ask your partner what you can say or do that really feels loving. That's the focus of our next exercise. Note that we're only going to ask about what you might do here, not what you might say, but the same principle applies in each area.

## The "Honey, I need you to teach me what I can do that will help you feel loved" Questionnaire

Your job is to bring this questionnaire to your partner, ask him or her to fill it out, and then meet with your partner to go over the results very carefully. Then, of course, you will want to use the information to give your partner the gifts he or she really wants.

Please rank the following gift possibilities from 1 to 15, with 1 being the gift you would most like to receive, 2 being the second-best gift, and so on. The idea here is to help your partner show his or her love for you in the ways you most want it, so please be honest and clear. Remember that your partner isn't a mind reader, so you need to tell him or her what you want in order to get it. We've left two spaces open for you to add your own ideas. Be sure to fill them in and rank them along with the rest.

_____ Make me one of my favorite meals.

_____ Take the children off my hands for a whole day.

_____ Give me a back rub (that doesn't lead to sex).

_____ Give me a hug or an embrace when I'm feeling anxious, frustrated, or depressed.

_____ Clean up the living room without my help.

_____ Give me a small gift for no reason.

_____ Take a walk with me without the kids.

_____ Go away with me for a weekend on the town.

_____ Work with me on a big project (such as painting the house).

_____ Go dancing with me.

_____ Take me out for dinner.

_____ Make love to me in a special way I like.

_____ Spend an entire day with me and the kids.

_____ _____. (Put your own suggestion here)

_____ _____. (Put your own suggestion here)

When you have completed your questionnaire, please return it to your partner. He or she may want to talk it over with you, perhaps asking for details about what you want, maybe wanting to learn more about why the things you ranked highest help you feel loved.

# Do something generous for your partner

One of the best ways to show love to your partner is by being generous. That means going a little out of your way to do something nice for him or her, something that you don't have to do and is not expected or demanded. Acts of generosity are most often small things like bringing your partner a slice of pizza from that restaurant he or she really likes or doing the dishes even though it's not your turn. But sometimes acts of generosity are far bigger than that: buying an airplane ticket so she can visit her pregnant daughter in Germany, accepting the stray dog he has fallen in love with, agreeing to move to a bigger house even though you are content with the one you have.

What does it mean to be generous? Dictionary definitions include "unselfish," "liberal in giving or sharing," "free from meanness or small-ness of mind," "giving to others something of value," "being warm and sympathetic to others," and "a readiness to give." Interestingly, two of the antonyms of generosity are "stinginess" and "pettiness." These words signal a certain smallness of character, a hanging on to whatever one has. Generosity is the exact opposite of that kind of smallness. The generous person shares his or her wealth and becomes a better person because of it.

Don't think of generosity as a sacrifice. The generous person wants to give to others. It feels good, not bad. So the generous individual doesn't

> **SMART SAYING**
>
> *Poor people share with the heart.*
> —HAITIAN SAYING

feel resentful or sigh with the burden of giving. He or she doesn't expect the other person to feel guilty or obligated to give something in return.

One more thing: the truly generous person does not give to another with an expectation of getting something back. A really generous gift always comes with no strings attached. The message is, "Here, take this. I want you to have it. I don't want or expect anything in return. You don't owe me anything. It just makes me happy to be able to give this to you."

Maybe you already think of yourself as a reasonably generous person. But almost everybody can learn to be a little more generous. Here's an exercise that will help you do just that.

First, see if you can think of a time when you were not generous with your partner. The format to use goes like this:

Last _____ [yesterday, last week, a month ago, etc.], I could have been generous with my partner by _____

_____

_____

_____

But I passed up that opportunity. Instead, I _____

_____

_____

_____

When I think about it, I believe I wasn't generous because _____

_____

_____

_____

If that same situation ever comes up again, I will _____

_____

_____

_____

Now think of a time when you were generous with your partner, a time when you gave him or her something (a gift, your time, etc.) you didn't have to just because it felt good to do so.

Last _____ [yesterday, last week, a month ago, etc.], I noticed an opportunity to be generous with my partner. Here's what I did: _____

_____

_____

Here's what I thought and felt when I did that: _____

_____

_____

_____

If the same opportunity came up again, I would _____

_____

_____

_____

Now see if you can think of three to five ways you could be generous with your partner in the immediate future.

In the next few days I could be generous with my partner by:

_____

and by _____

and by _____

and by _____

and by _____

Come back to this page in about a week and see how many times you did manage to be generous by doing the things you wrote about above or in other ways.

# Unexpected surprises add romance to your relationship

It's not the dozen roses on his or her birthday that counts the most. It's the single rose you pick up on the way home one night for no reason at all. And the little note on the pillow saying "I love you." And the offer to take the kids to the zoo so your partner can have some needed alone time this weekend. And the gentle hug you give as he or she is passing by. And all those other small, unexpected acts of kindness, thoughtfulness, and generosity that surprise your partner. These are the gifts that tell your partner that you are always thinking about him or her. They also convey the message that you really want your partner to feel loved and cared about every day. Think of these little signs of consideration as the icing on the cake of love. They help the whole cake taste sweeter and look better. There's one more reason, though, to give unexpected surprises to your partner. Perhaps this is the best reason of all: *unexpected surprises help keep the romance in your relationship.*

What does it mean when people use the word *romantic*? Well, some of the dictionary definitions and synonyms of romantic include: "fanciful," "impractical," "unrealistic," "idealistic," "adventuresome," "extravagant," "imaginative," "colorful," "chivalrous," and "fantastic." The opposites of romantic are listed as "practical" and "realistic." Now, there's certainly nothing wrong with being practical and realistic, as long as you aren't that

Smart Humor

A kiss on the nose

A nip on the ear

A warm sweater

A pat on the rear

A thing that's small

Or out of routine

A playful pun

A nectarine

A soft massage

Upon your shoulder

Makes you warm

Instead of colder

—PATRICIA
POTTER-EFRON

way all the time. But all too often relationships become far too practical and realistic over time. Quite frankly, relationships get stale when they become too predictable. Still, it's often hard to create space for lengthy romantic interludes such as a week off in the Bahamas. That's where these unexpected surprises come in. They help keep the romance in your relationship every day, making the relationship both less predictable and more enjoyable.

So what's the recipe for this romantic icing on the cake of love? Try this combination.

- *Spontaneity*—doing nice things on the spur of the moment without a lot of planning.

- *Thoughtfulness*—knowing the small things that your partner really appreciates.

- *Playfulness*—surprising your partner with stuff that gets a laugh.

- *Adventurousness*—being willing to try something even if you're not sure how much your partner will appreciate it.

- *Unpredictability*—breaking the mold by giving a gift or doing something for your partner you've never done before.

One caution: spontaneity is not the same as impulsiveness. Don't suddenly spend $20,000 on a ring the size of Colorado. That's romantic only in the eyes of your credit card company. Also note that many pleasant surprises don't involve buying a gift. Instead, they are about your saying or doing something nice for your partner.

Here's a set of fill in the blanks that might help you get better at surprising your partner with romantic gifts.

If I had $5 today to buy my partner a surprise small gift I would get him or her a _____.

A food item I've never brought my partner that I bet he or she would enjoy is a _____.

I guess my partner would really be pleasantly surprised if I gave him or her

a _____.

My partner would burst out laughing if I brought home a _____

_____.

Something nice about my partner I've never told him or her is _____

_____.

I could offer to _____

for my partner today or this weekend. That would be a nice surprise.

My partner would be pleasantly embarrassed if I showed up wearing a

T-shirt that said _____

[a message such as "I'm totally in love with _____"].

Something else I could say or do that would be an unexpected surprise

for my partner would be to _____

_____.

# Keep "I love you" special: Don't misuse or overuse the words

Marty is good at saying "I love you" to his partner, Freddy. In fact, he proclaims his love several times a day. The problem is that he often uses that phrase as part of an excuse, as in "I'm sorry, Freddy. I forgot to pick up the groceries. But I love you." He also uses "I love you" to get what he wants: "Freddy, I love you so much. Say, you wouldn't happen to have a few extra dollars on you, would you? I need gas money."

Georgianna must say "I love you" a hundred times a day. "I love you, pass the butter." "I love you, nice weather we're having, isn't it?" "I love you, I love you, I love you, I love you . . . " Her family no longer even hears those words. They've lost their emotional impact.

"I love you" is probably the single most important statement anyone can make. Those words are powerful, compelling, compassionate, and exciting. Certainly most of the exercises in this book are meant to help people say them more often. However, "I love you" can be misused (like by Marty) or overused (like by Georgianna).

Keep these guidelines in mind.

- Do say "I love you" frequently. Remember that this phrase is a wonderful gift you can give your partner. Nothing is gained by not saying "I love you" when you feel love. So don't be stingy with your words.

> **SMART SAYING**
>
> *Words and hearts should be handled with care For words when spoken and hearts when broken Are the hardest things to repair.*
> —ANONYMOUS

- Mean it when you say it. Now, you may be angry at or unhappy with your partner and still say "I love you" to him or her. You don't have to be happy to feel loving. But it is important that you feel, if only for an instant, the special sensations that come with really loving someone. Be sure to take a little time to feel the truth in your words as you say them.

- Keep your actions consistent with the idea of love. Be sure to match your words with your deeds. Loving actions are the perfect complement to loving words.

- Don't say "I love you" only out of habit. If it doesn't mean anything to you, it won't mean much to your partner, either.

- Don't say "I love you" to get something you want. Do that very often and you'll soon hear this response: "Oh, sure you love me. So what do you want this time?"

- Don't pair the phrase "I love you" with criticism or negativity. Saying things like "It's only because I love you that I'm telling you that you need to lose weight [get a job, quit drinking]" contaminates the phrase.

How about you? How often do you do the following: Answer with never, once in a great while, fairly often, or quite frequently.

1. Forget to say "I love you" when you could? _____

2. Say "I love you" but don't take the time to feel it? _____

3. Say "I love you" but act as if you don't? _____

4. Say "I love you" to get something you want? _____

5. Say "I love you" simply out of habit? _____

6. Say "I love you" but pair that phrase with negativity or criticism? _____

Here's a suggested assignment.

We just mentioned six problems regarding the underuse, overuse, and misuse of the phrase "I love you." Select the problem that most weakens your relationship—the one that most keeps your partner from feeling deeply loved. Then make a personal commitment to alter that behavior.

The repair formulas are, of course, the polar opposites of the problem.

- If the problem is that you forget to say "I love you" when you could, then you need to make a commitment to say "I love you" more often. There are several exercises in this book that can help you do that.

- If the problem is that you say "I love you" but don't take the time to feel it, then you need to slow down, breathe, and sense that emotion. You need to focus on quality more than quantity here, feeling the impact of each "I love you" on your body, mind, and soul.

- If the problem is that you say "I love you" but act as if you don't, then you need to begin treating your partner with greater respect, caring, consideration, and thoughtfulness. Otherwise all you are giving is the illusion of love—wrapping paper without anything real inside.

- If the problem is that you say "I love you" to get something you want, then you must quit running that particular con game. Stop trying to manipulate your partner. Love is about caring for your partner, not using him or her. It may be difficult to stop this behavior, especially if it's worked in the past. Ultimately, though, it will be worth the effort if you want to experience the feeling of real love. Practice saying "I love you" without asking for, wanting, or expecting anything.

- If the problem is that you say "I love you" simply out of habit, then try cutting out that phrase completely for a few days. Notice all the times you normally would say "I love you" automatically, without real feeling, but don't say it. Then, after you have abstained for a while, begin saying "I love you," but ration yourself at first to no more than twice a day to any single person. Take the time to feel your love every time you say it.

- If the problem is that you say "I love you" but pair that phrase with negativity or criticism, then never, ever follow that sentence with the word "but" (as in, "I love you, but you did that all wrong") or any other form of criticism. If you do feel a need to be critical or negative (everybody does from time to time, but we hope you don't overdo it), then just go ahead and say what you have to say without any reference to love.

Keep love special. Use the phrase "I love you" well.

# Follow the accordion model of a loving relationship: Recognize the value of both closeness and temporary separation

Love, for some couples, feels like a waltz played by a string quartet. For others, it's a hard rock concert featuring electric guitars, a square dance complete with fiddlers, or a soulful ballad. But one instrument that often reminds us of a loving partnership is an accordion. Why? Because of the way the bellows of the accordion, first filling up with air in order to be able to make notes and then contracting as the sounds emerge, resembles the way that loving couples handle their needs for closeness and temporary separation in their relationship.

One of the areas in a partnership that every couple must negotiate is distancing. Questions like the ones below must be asked and answered, usually not just once but many times over the length of the relationship.

- Do we want to spend time together today?

- Is it okay to want to get away from each other for a little while?

- Will I hurt your feelings if today I want to take some time with my friends instead of being with you?

SMART THOUGHT

- Does one of us generally want more closeness than the other?

If you want to tune up your relationship

And one wants to be close, the other far away,

Try this:

If you seem always far away

Then I'll quit chasing you

And wait instead of blowing up

And threatening the worst.

If you seem always close to me

I'll not run out of here

I'll stay instead of leaving

And still my fear.

Most people have times when they want to get really close to their partner. These are the times when they desire to share meaningful conversation, make love, walk side by side. The message they convey to their partner at these moments is "I'm glad we're together." However, these same people also will feel a desire to spend some time apart from their partner. That's when they want to be alone or with others. The message they convey to their partner at these times is "Right now I need some distance."

Meanwhile, their partners have the same needs for closeness and distance. So at any one time there are four distinct possibilities:

1. I want closeness and you want closeness.

2. I want distance and you want distance.

3. I want closeness and you want distance.

4. I want distance and you want closeness.

Now, the first two situations are easy to deal with. The accordion makes great music without a note of disharmony. You and your partner smoothly connect for a while or spend some time away from each other by mutual consent. In fact, those two options might follow each other. Imagine, for instance, a couple that makes intense love and then happily drifts off into separate rooms to read, write, or work apart.

But what about the latter two situations? One of you wants closeness and the other distance. What's going to happen? Will one of you end up feeling smothered because the other insists on too much togetherness? Will one of you feel isolated and lonely because the other refuses to get close? How can one accordion play decent music when two people are trying to get it to do different things?

There are two keys to dealing with this issue: personal awareness and mutual discussion/negotiation.

## Personal Awareness

We'd like you to write a brief statement about your desire for closeness and distance in your relationship. Please mention in this paragraph what you know about your needs for closeness and distance in your relationship; how you notice when you want closeness and when you want distance; how you let your partner know about your desire for closeness or distance; and any changes you'd like to encourage about how much closeness or distance there is in your relationship.

_____

_____

_____

_____

_____

## Mutual Discussion/Negotiation

Here are five ideas that will help you discuss and negotiate distancing issues with your partner.

1. Both closeness and separation are normal and necessary in any healthy relationship.

2. It's okay to speak up for your needs for closeness and distance. It's okay for your partner to speak up as well. There is no right or wrong here, just natural differences that must be accepted.

3. Getting close doesn't mean you'll get smothered. You can create distance when you need it.

4. Taking time apart doesn't mean the relationship is bad or weak. Have faith that both of you will want to reconnect after spending time away from each other.

5. You will be able to meet both of your needs for closeness and separation most of the time if you keep talking.

So, if you are doing this exercise with your partner, please take the time to read what you just wrote out loud to your partner. Listen carefully to your partner's statement, too. Discuss how you can give each other clear signals when you want time together or apart. Talk about any fears either of you might have about getting too close or too distant. See if you can remember times when one of you wanted closeness and the other distance. How did you handle those situations? How could you handle them better in the future?

If you are doing this exercise alone, think about how you have handled your own need for closeness and separation in past and current relationships. Also think about how you've dealt with your partners' needs for closeness and separation. Then think about how you can use this knowledge to enhance your current or future relationships.

# There must be fifty ways to love a leaver: Helping the partner who runs from closeness

In just about every relationship one person is a little more comfortable showing affection than the other. That's normal. But in some relationships the difference is huge. One partner is full of love and wants to show it a lot. Meanwhile, the other partner holds back, shying away both from giving and receiving messages of love. That person acts as if he or she were born with internal love deflectors designed to keep out intimacy. And if those deflectors don't work well enough, sometimes that person just flat out runs away from love, fleeing to the television set, the garage, or the shopping center. In terms of adult attachment style this partner is usually either Dismissive ("I am independent—I don't need anybody's love") or Fearful ("I'm scared to take in love—I feel too vulnerable when I do"). Many of the exercises in this book are designed to help these love deflectors learn how to express and receive love messages. But not this one.

We've written this exercise for those of you who are frustrated because your partner is a love deflector. You try to tell your partner how much you love him or her. Unfortunately, your partner seems not to notice your efforts, fails to respond lovingly, runs away, or even angrily rejects your love offerings. At those times you might catch yourself thinking something

> **SMART SAYING**
>
> *Be not afraid of going slowly;*
> *Be afraid only of standing still.*
> —CHINESE PROVERB

**147**

like, "Why do I bother trying to show my partner my love when all I get back is a shrug? What's the use?" Remember, though, your partner probably really wants to feel your love. It's just that he or she isn't very good at it. Maybe your partner grew up in an unloving or undemonstrative home. Perhaps your partner is gun-shy because he or she suffered many rejections or betrayals in the past. Whatever the reason, you're in this relationship together, so you might as well keep trying to express your love. Some of your love is bound to get through those deflectors. Then your partner will realize that being loved is a wonderful feeling.

Here's a simple formula to follow with your love-shy partner: Be accepting of your partner's limitations. Be patient. Be creative.

- *Be accepting of your partner's limitations.* Your partner is scared of intimacy. That's a reality. So if you push too hard, too fast, or too long, your partner will be overwhelmed. That's when he or she will put up the deflector or run away. You'll have to be gentle in your approach and be willing to back away if any particular idea doesn't work. Above all, don't demand, lecture, guilt-trip, or beg for love.

- *Be patient.* Have faith that the strength of your love will gradually overcome your partner's fears. This will take time, though. Not days but months and years. However, people do change, and partners who are afraid of intimacy can learn to take in love at deeper and deeper levels. Look for signs of progress over time, such as your partner gradually going from saying, "Uh-huh" when you say "I love you" to responding with, "I love you, too" to actually saying "I love you" first.

- *Be creative.* That's where the title of this exercise comes in (with a little help from the songwriter Paul Simon). The idea is to look for subtle ways to show your love that don't automatically trigger your partner's love deflector. Here are fifty suggestions. Check the ones that might work for you with your partner.

  ____ 1. Tuck a "By the way, I love you" note into your partner's purse, schoolbag, or briefcase.

  ____ 2. Give your partner an unexpected small gift such as a mug with his or her name on it.

____ 3. Touch your partner softly on the arm to convey your love.

____ 4. Offer your partner a back rub or a massage.

____ 5. Suggest going to a movie that you know is special for your partner.

____ 6. Lean over and whisper "I love you" without expecting a response.

____ 7. Play "your" song on the CD player.

____ 8. Make your partner's favorite meal.

____ 9. Help your partner with a job that he or she normally does alone.

____ 10. Bring your partner a cup of coffee when he or she is engrossed in a task.

____ 11. Tell your partner that he or she is special.

____ 12. Praise your partner when he or she expresses love to you or the kids.

____ 13. Read the paper beside your partner instead of in the other room.

____ 14. Say, "It's okay when you don't answer me when I say 'I love you.' I still love you."

____ 15. Repeat your love messages if your partner doesn't seem to hear you the first time.

____ 16. Ask your partner what he or she is thinking about when he or she is quiet.

____ 17. Take the initiative to create times when the two of you can be together.

____ 18. Sit next to your partner and do your own thing.

____ 19. Whisper "sweet nothings" in your partner's ear.

____ 20. Say "I love you" playfully instead of seriously.

____ 21. Ask your partner what is scary about being in love and just listen.

___ 22. Put a blanket around your partner on a cold day.

___ 23. Go to a house of worship together and then talk about the sermon.

___ 24. Write a poem about your love for your partner.

___ 25. Ask your partner about what he or she really wants in life.

___ 26. Ask your partner what love means to him or her.

___ 27. Ask your partner what you do that helps him or her feel loved.

___ 28. Tell your partner when something he or she does makes you feel loved.

___ 29. Reach over and hold your partner's hand on a walk.

___ 30. Hold hands in public if that isn't too embarrassing for your partner.

___ 31. Reassure your partner that you are sticking around.

___ 32. Thank your partner just for being a good person.

___ 33. Call for a couple minutes in the middle of your busy day.

___ 34. Share a good joke together so you can hear each other's laughter.

___ 35. Let your partner go away without making him or her feel guilty.

___ 36. Kiss your partner on the top of the head.

___ 37. Throw in an "I love you" when it's least expected.

___ 38. Send flowers.

___ 39. Ask your partner how love was expressed in his or her family.

___ 40. Notice and mention how your partner shows you love without saying "I love you."

___ 41. In your partner's presence, tell others how and why you love your partner.

___ 42. Reromanticize your love life by making a special effort to seduce your partner.

___ 43. Tell your partner you can feel his or her love for you and that it feels good.

___ 44. Remind your partner that he or she is loved "just in case you forgot."

___ 45. Give your partner a quick hug.

___ 46. Gently encourage your partner to go ahead and say "I love you" more often.

___ 47. Reassure your insecure partner that he or she is loved and lovable.

___ 48. Create a secret "I love you" message that you can share without others knowing.

___ 49. Take time to show appreciation when your partner does say "I love you."

___ 50. Ask your partner to turn off his or her love deflectors for a few minutes.

# PART THREE

# How to Take In Love

# Make a promise to yourself to take in your partner's love and affection

Sixty years of research in the area of parent-child attachment validates one theme: human beings are internally hardwired to receive nurturance from other human beings. Actually, we're programmed to demand nurturance, as anyone who's ever tried to ignore a hungry infant for a few minutes can attest. Indeed, we begin life anything but helpless. Infants are born with a "Take care of me—now!" signal system that generally works quite effectively. Women (and we think some men, too) are biologically programmed to respond to an infant's needs. Otherwise, what good would it do for the infant to cry?

Gradually, infants respond to the parent answering their cry not just by quitting crying but with a smile. They recognize their parents' faces. A special bond develops that changes "I'm any baby being taken care of by any mother" into "I'm a unique child being taken care of by my one and only one mommy." That's how "Feed me" evolves into "Love me." From a child's point of view, then, you can't separate being loved from being nurtured. To a child, it's completely normal, natural, and necessary to take in another's love.

Life gets a little more complex by the time we reach adulthood. The

155

nurturing in adult romantic relationships usually is two-directional. Each partner both gives and receives nurturance from the other. (Not always in equal amounts, though. One common complaint we hear in marriage counseling is that one person thinks he or she gives way more than 50 percent to the other. More often than not, in American society, it is the woman who feels overburdened and undernurtured.) In addition, adults have a very wide range of wants and needs. It's no longer just "Feed me" but "Feed me and hold me and make love to me and spend time with me and talk with me and listen to me and tell me you love me." Our main point, though, is almost the same as before: just as with children, *it's natural, normal, and necessary for adults to take in their partner's love.*

Somewhere along the path of life, however, some people may have lost touch with this simple truth. If that has happened to you, then you shy away from taking in nurturing and love. In particular, you often ignore, decline, or reject your partner's attempts to take care of you. Perhaps you grew up in a home where you didn't observe much love-giving or love-taking, so it doesn't seem right to want that now. Or maybe you were told that people should only give and never receive. Whatever the reasons, today you realize that you don't take in a lot of the love that your partner offers you. Consciously or unconsciously, you commonly deliver a "No, thanks, dear" message to your partner. "No, thanks; I don't want your caring. No, thanks; I don't need your tenderness. No, thanks; I won't take your comfort. No, thanks; I can't take your love."

We have other exercises in this section designed to help you figure out how and why you defend against taking love. Those exercises will help you understand and challenge the sources of your discomfort about taking love in. But here we aren't as interested in those things. Instead, we hope you give yourself permission to take in your partner's love. We believe that almost anyone reading this book can make a clear, conscious choice to take in their partner's love. It's basically up to you. Nobody can make you take in love, caring, and kindness. You can block it forever. But why would you want to? Declining to take in your partner's love makes about as much sense as refusing to eat at a banquet or rejecting a warm blanket on the coldest day of the year. All that goodness is right there. All you have to do is receive it. So accept it. Now.

There's not much writing involved with this exercise. All you have to do is sign your name to the promise suggested below. However, we ask that you not just quickly sign and dash off to the next exercise. Please take the time to think your promise through.

Ask yourself these questions: What would it really mean to me if I let myself fully take in my partner's love? How might doing so affect me? How might it impact my partner? Am I really ready to make this promise to myself? Can I carry it through? Am I signing because I think I should or because I actually want to? Is this my free choice that doesn't feel like a duty, sacrifice, or burden?

Here's the promise.

> *Beginning today I promise to make a clear and conscious effort to take in my partner's love. I will quit ignoring, declining, or rejecting my partner's acts of love, kindness, caring, and consideration. Instead, I will let myself accept these signs of love. Not only will I accept my partner's love, I will feel that person's love deep within me.*

Signed _____Date_____

# Put your "no" on the shelf: Choosing to let in your partner's love

You are indeed fortunate if you have somebody in your life who tells you that he or she loves you and does loving things for you. However, those acts of kindness and caring are only good for you if you can take them in. If you have developed habits that keep you from accepting those words and acts of love, then they are pretty much wasted.

Here are a few ways in which people avoid love. Check off the ones that you do most frequently.

_____ Fail to notice the nice things their partner has said or done for them.

_____ Not respond in any way when told they are loved.

_____ Start an argument to keep their partner at a distance.

_____ Stay too busy to have time for that love stuff.

_____ Take care of their partner but don't let him or her care for them.

_____ Put their energy into a hundred friendships but don't let anyone, not even their partner, get really close.

\_\_\_ Shrug off statements of love with an "uh-huh, that's nice" without really feeling the love.

\_\_\_ Carry around resentments about how their partner has hurt them in the past so they don't have to believe that he or she is loving them today.

\_\_\_ Doubt that their partner could really love them because they don't really love themselves.

\_\_\_ Confuse taking in love with feeling obligated to do things for their partner—that's when "I love you" gets confused with "Yeah, so what do you want from me now?"

\_\_\_ Play the "Yes, I hear you love me, but do you really, really love me?" game.

There may be many reasons you have trouble saying yes to love. Family-of-origin problems. Unhappy past relationships. Broken dreams. Whatever your reasons, one thing is certain: you have developed a habit of turning down opportunities to feel loved. In fact, you'd probably feel wonderful if you would let yourself say yes to love instead of no. Here's what you can do to challenge that habit.

- Imagine that the word *no* is written on an old familiar hat that you automatically reach for every morning to place upon your head.

- Now imagine that you've just received a brand-new, really nice hat that says yes on it instead of no.

- Your job is to remember to put on the "yes" hat every morning. Also, keep checking during the day to see if you've temporarily misplaced that new hat. If you can keep the "yes" hat on your head, you will be ready to receive love when it is offered.

- Keep that "no" hat on the shelf. But don't worry about losing it. You'll always be able to take it back off the shelf if you really need it.

Obviously, you have a choice every morning, afternoon, and evening about which hat to select. And, believe us, it makes a huge difference which one you choose. The "no" hat leads to isolation, defensiveness, loneliness, and dismissiveness. The "yes" hat leads to contact, warmth, and feeling loved.

Here's your assignment: take one minute every morning to select your hat for the day. You can certainly choose your old familiar "no" hat if you desire. Just be sure to tell yourself exactly why you are doing that. On the other hand, you may decide to select the "yes" hat. If so, then keep it on your head. Think about what taking in love means to you and remember all day to let love in.

# The five steps that let you take in love

It's one thing to want to take in love but another to be able to do so. This exercise is designed to help you with the actual mechanics of receiving your partner's love, caring, respect, and admiration. Taking in love will be relatively easy if you follow this clear and direct process. There are only five steps.

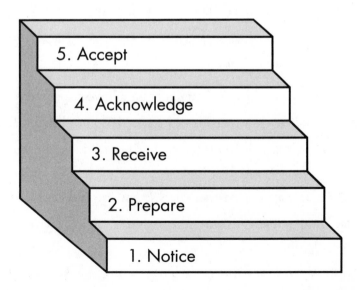

*Step One: Notice That Someone Is Showing You Love*

Imagine that you've been walking in a fog. You couldn't see much of anything, but now the fog is lifting. That's when you notice somebody approaching. It's your partner (or anyone else who loves you). Your partner is saying something, but you can't quite make out the words. You focus in a little, paying more attention, until you can make them out: "I love you." Wow. You weren't expecting that, but there it is.

Congratulations! You've just begun the process of taking in love. But so far all that's happened is that you've heard the words. You still need to do four more things to really take them into your heart.

*Step Two: Prepare to Take in Love*

This is the point at which you quickly remind yourself that you want to take in that love. You stop yourself from deflecting the love (by ignoring it, starting a fight, changing the subject, suddenly getting busy, running away, etc.). You dismiss any thoughts like "I don't deserve to be loved" or "This can't be real." You focus on one thing: giving yourself permission to accept being loved. You'll think something like, "My partner [or someone else] is telling me I am loved. This time I'm ready to feel it."

*Step Three: Receive Love*

In this step, you physically and mentally take in your partner's love.

- Breathe! Take a slow, deep breath. That lets your body feel loved.

- Listen to those words with your entire mind, totally attending to them.

- Look directly at your partner's eyes so you can meet each other's souls.

- Relax. Taking love in is wonderful, so you might as well relax instead of tensing up.

- Feel the warmth in your body. That's a physical response to the feeling of safety that goes with taking in love.

- Touch or hold the person who loves you. That helps your whole body feel loved.

- Take your time. Feeling loved is one of life's wonderful luxuries. So don't rush off to do the dishes. Let that feeling of being loved soak in.

- Believe in yourself and your partner. This really is happening. You are being loved, right now. Take that love in.

## Step Four: Acknowledge That You Feel Loved

This step is important because you are validating what just happened. You do this in two ways. The first is to tell yourself in your own words this thought: "I just let myself feel loved. That felt _____." We hope the first word that comes to mind is "great" or "wonderful." But it's okay if taking in love felt scary or weird or silly. Just be honest with yourself.

The second way to acknowledge being loved is to say something out loud to your partner. You can thank him or her. You can share your feeling response. Don't, though, automatically say "I love you" to your partner if saying that would distract you from your own feelings. There will be plenty of time later to give some loving back. Recognize that your partner wants you to enjoy the experience of feeling loved, so you don't have to apologize or feel guilty about being the recipient this time.

## Step Five: Accept That You Are Loved

This is the afterglow stage. You let yourself think about being loved. You notice your thoughts and feelings a few minutes later, an hour later, a few hours after, the next day. You accept that you are a loved human being. You are both loved and lovable. What a miracle. What a trip. What a deal. It's actually true. You are loved. Keep that feeling of being loved real in your mind, body, heart and soul. That helps you get ready for the next time someone tells you that you are loved.

Please review the five steps we just described. Then answer these questions.

Which of the five steps is easiest for you? _____

Which step is hardest? _____

Why? _____

## Step One (Notice)

How do you keep from noticing when people are trying to tell you that you are loved? _____

_____

How can you learn to pay more attention at those times? _____

_____

_____

## Step Two (Prepare)

What do you *do* that keeps you from focusing on taking in love?

_____

_____

What do you *think* that keeps you from taking in love? _____

_____

_____

What do you most need to *do* to prepare to take in another's love when it is offered? _____

_____

What do you most need to *think* to prepare to take in another's love when it is offered? _____

_____

## Step Three (Receive)

What two or three things from the list on pages 164–165 would most help you take in love? _____

_____

Can you think of anything else not on our list that would help?

_____

_____

## Step Four (Acknowledge)

What's a good way for you to acknowledge to yourself that you are loved? _____

_____

What's a good way for you to acknowledge to others that you are loved?

_____

_____

## Step Five (Accept)

Say this sentence to yourself a few minutes after you've taken in some love: "I am loved and lovable." How does that feel? _____

_____

_____

Repeat that sentence in one hour, two hours, the next day. Notice your feelings and thoughts as you do so. Write them down here.

One hour later: _____

_____

Two hours later: _____

_____

Next day: _____

_____

# Take in love one small bit at a time to avoid feeling overwhelmed

The immediate feeling of being loved can be a tremendously intense experience. Your partner says "I love you" and somehow you feel like crying, your body tingles with energy, you feel warm all over. You want to shout with joy, give your partner a hug—or run away.

Some people find it hard to take in love at first because it feels overwhelming. Some of these people may have felt smothered by a parent or a partner in the past. Others mistakenly connect feeling loved with a sense of obligation or guilt, as if being loved creates a debt you must repay. Still others have shut themselves down and are afraid to open up to love because they have been badly hurt in the past. These people don't like the feeling of vulnerability that accompanies love. Finally, some individuals shy away from taking in love because they fear losing control over their feelings or actions.

The common denominator for all these people is that they feel overwhelmed by love. The sensation of being loved is just too scary, powerful, or intense. "Run," they say to themselves. "Hide. Get away from this feeling." And so they run or hide. They ignore the comment, leave the room,

SMART HABIT

Make taking in love as much of a habit as brushing your teeth.

**169**

change the subject, look away, laugh it off, or pick a fight. But they usually don't run too far away because they really do want to feel loved.

So what can you do if you are someone who shies away from the intense sensations of being loved? *The answer is to take in love a little bit at a time.* Try a nibble instead of a mouthful. Turn the music on halfway instead of full blast. Light a candle to your heart but not a five-hundred-watt bulb. That way you can stay in control. You won't get overpowered. You stay in charge of your mind and body. But at the same time you are learning better how to take in love. Eventually, you'll be able to eat an entire meal instead of just one bite. You'll be able to listen to louder music. You'll see love in a stronger light. But it's okay to start with a simple goal: to take in your partner's love one small bit at a time.

So what do we mean by taking in love one small bit at a time? When your partner says "I love you":

- It's okay to only glance briefly at your partner, but don't avoid all eye contact.

- It's okay to only briefly answer ("Uh-huh, thanks"), but not to completely ignore your partner.

- It's okay to hug your partner lightly, but not to stiffen against his or her touch.

- It's okay to leave in a minute, but not to bolt out the door.

- It's okay to say "I love you, too," but not so quickly that you avoid feeling loved.

- It's okay to wonder how anyone would ever want to love you, but not to refuse to believe it.

- It's okay to breathe normally, but not to hold your breath.

- It's okay to notice your fear of taking in love, but not to give in to it.

Obviously the idea is to take in what you can, enjoy it, and then come back for more.

Now it's your turn. Please complete the following sentences.

Taking in love one small bit at a time is important to me because

_____

_____

When my partner expresses love for me, I will remember that it is okay
for me to _____
as long as I don't _____

When I start to feel overwhelmed by my partner's love for me, I will

_____

Right now I feel I can take in about _____ percent of my partner's love.
I would like to be able to take in _____ percent by this time next week. I
would like to be able to take in _____ percent by this time next month, and
_____ percent by this time next year.

In order for me to take in a little more love from my partner than I have
been able to, I will _____

_____

# You can't take in what you don't see: Notice the times when your partner is caring and considerate

They're right there, waiting for you to observe. The coffee that's ready for you when you wake up. That call just to say hello while you are at work. A rental movie that is exactly the type you like most. Kind words. A playful touch on your arm. The extra time with the kids so you can finish your nap. Something special said or done during lovemaking that makes you feel really good. A small gift given for no reason. Each of these things is your partner's way of saying "I think about you a lot, I want you to be happy, and I love you."

But what if you don't notice these gifts? Perhaps you've never paid attention to such acts of kindness and consideration. Or maybe lately you're too busy thinking about something else. Not noticing, you fail to acknowledge them or to thank your partner. That's no big deal when it happens once in a while. But eventually you will pay a heavy price for your inattention. Unrewarded, your partner will begin cutting back on those nice words and deeds.

**SMART PRINCIPLE**

Love is forgetting to keep score.

Your first job, then, with this exercise is to notice the little ways in which your partner says "I love you." Your second task is to acknowledge them with a clear and direct "Thank you."

### Notice the Nice Things Your Partner Says and Does

Right now, today, begin looking for all the nice things your partner says or does for you. (Don't keep score, though, so you can complain that there aren't enough or that you are doing more. Just notice them.) Think of yourself as a telescope constantly scanning the universe for signs of life, except you are seeking one special type of life form, namely your partner's loving actions. Set your mind's telescope to "on" and keep it there. Remember that in the matter of love you will only find what you're looking for.

### Thank Your Partner for Those Nice Words and Actions

Begin thanking your partner for those kind words and acts. Don't overdo it. A simple "thank you" is usually enough to let your partner know you've noticed what he or she has just done.

# How to avoid the slide into defensiveness (only looking for the bad stuff)

We've mentioned before that we are marriage counselors. Sadly, it's often during couples sessions that we get lessons on what goes wrong in relationships. We call one very predictable pattern the "slide into defensiveness." This slide happens when troubled and anxious people begin watching only for their partner's criticisms, negative comments, or other attacks. They are so concerned about defending against the next attack that they stay on constant alert. They behave like soldiers guarding the perimeter of their territory, ignoring anything that isn't threatening so that their entire energy can focus on survival. Sometimes these frightened soldiers even begin firing at shadows, convinced that the enemy must be out there.

But your partner isn't an enemy soldier.[*] He or she isn't loading a weapon right now as you read this book. In fact, your partner may be heading your way with a cool glass of lemonade or a cup of tea intended just for you.

---

[*]We realize that some of you live with partners who may indeed be physically or emotionally dangerous. If your partner really has become the enemy, we urge you to get help or get out. However, we assume here, and elsewhere in this book, that your partner is generally a good person who wants you to feel safe.

SMART THOUGHT

When you were growing up, did you ever play the game Chutes and Ladders? Well, the chutes that plunge a relationship back to the start are called negativity, hopelessness, pessimism, and despair. The ladders that take a couple to victory are named optimism, hope, creativity, and love. So why don't you see if you can find one or more of those ladders to climb today.

We understand that most people become defensive for a reason. Perhaps your partner has said some really mean things to you that are hard to forget. Maybe you have felt set up because what started out as a compliment turned into a criticism ("Honey, thanks for doing the laundry, but you forgot to take the clothes out of the dryer and now they're all wrinkled. You never do anything right, do you?"). So you've become negative about the entire relationship. Okay, that's understandable. But now you have a choice. Will you continue to be defensive, to assume the worst about your partner, *or* will you give him or her the benefit of the doubt and quit being so defensive? If you want to take the second option, do these things:

- Keep looking for the good things your partner does (see exercise 35).

- Consciously remind yourself not to be defensive.

- If you do notice that you are becoming defensive, take a deep breath or two and let that defensiveness float out of your system.

- Tell yourself this: "I know my partner is on my side. He (or she) is not the enemy so I shouldn't treat him (or her) that way."

- Make a list of everything you think, say, and do when you become defensive. Then make a new list of things that you can think, say, and do to quit being defensive. For instance, if you fold your arms tightly around your body when you get defensive, let your arms drop to your sides instead.

When I get defensive with my partner, here's what I

Think: _____

_____

Say: _____

_____

Do: _____

_____

Instead I will:

Think: _____

_____

Say: _____

_____

Do: _____

_____

# Give your partner opportunities to be loving

There are many people who don't tell their partners what they want because they think it would mean more if their partner figured it out without help. Their idea is that they would feel more loved if their partners knew them well enough to read their minds or could intuitively sense what they wanted or needed. "If you loved me," these people say, "you would know that . . ." But most of the time that's not true. Love does not automatically lead to understanding. Your partner can love you deeply and still not know about something you really want or need. Good partners don't necessarily think alike. And good partners certainly cannot be expected to be mind readers.

There is a general principle here that applies to many aspects of a relationship: *don't create tests for your partner to see if he or she really loves you.* When you do so only two things can happen: (1) your partner will fail the test and you'll feel unloved or (2) your partner will pass the test, so you'll create another until eventually he or she will fail the test and you'll feel unloved. Testing belongs in schools, not relationships.

On the other hand, *you can and should create opportunities for your partner to show caring and be loving.* But there is a big difference between giving your partner a test and giving him or her an opportunity. You can't fail opportunities. True, your partner might miss some opportunities to be

SMART THOUGHT

Remember, as you give your partner opportunities to be loving, that nobody is perfect. So let your partner be "good enough," not perfect. A good enough partner is someone who often but not always shows love when you offer the opportunity.

loving that you offer. Perhaps he could have brought you flowers for your birthday but forgot. Perhaps she could have showed a little more appreciation for the hard work you just did around the house. You'll probably feel a little disappointed when that happens. But you'll still feel loved. Besides, there will be more opportunities for your partner to show caring down the line.

Let's return to the matter of telling your partner what you want. If there is something important you want from your partner, you need to tell him or her about it. Telling your partner offers him or her an opportunity to respond. Not saying anything, though, creates one of those "If you love me, you . . ." tests that are a setup for resentment. So go ahead and mention that you want more alone time or more together time or more cuddling time or more shared activities or whatever else really matters to you.

Here is a place for you to write down any of your "If you love me, you . . ." tests. Be sure to think about this carefully as you start writing. Sometimes these love tests are partly subconscious. You have to be really honest with yourself so you can bring half-conscious material into full awareness. One way to identify these hidden tests is to remember times you wanted something badly from your partner but you didn't say anything. Or perhaps you hinted so vaguely that you created a guessing game or a puzzle that your partner couldn't solve. Or possibly you asked for something totally unreasonable that guaranteed your partner's failure. Or maybe you expected and even wanted your partner to fail so you could feel miserable. Make sure you write down any of these love test games that you are still playing. Those tests are the ones that you will want to eliminate immediately.

If you love me, you _____

If you love me, you _____

If you love me, you _____

If you love me, you _____

If you love me, you _____

What haven't you told your partner? Think about this for a day or two. Then make a short list of important things you want or need from your partner. If possible, ask your partner to do the same. Take an hour together to go through both lists. Just remember that you are offering your partner opportunities here. Don't set yourselves up for failure by turning these opportunities into tests.

# Practice taking in love every time you give it out: Breathe in silver and breathe out gold

Some readers of this workbook may find it easier to give love than to receive it. Others may be just the reverse, more comfortable taking in love than giving it out. But ultimately most people feel best when they achieve a balance between these two complementary aspects of human compassion. In this exercise, we describe a Buddhist approach to helping people discover and maintain balance in life. This exercise is particularly useful with regard to balancing taking in and giving out love.

The Buddhists know and understand a lot about breath and how breathing brings spirit into (inspires) the body, as well as how breath and body fit into the universe. One school of Buddhist thought is based on compassion. There is a particular breathing exercise this group of Buddhists likes to do. This exercise is not difficult, and as we master it we calm our spirit while increasing our ability both to receive and give love.

This exercise is called "breathe in silver, breathe out gold." Both silver and gold are precious. In one way, then, this exercise says: breathe in the best this world has to offer, then send it on as you exhale to nourish and nurture others. So think words like *loved*, *treasured*, and *cherished* as you

183

inhale, and as you exhale think words like *loving, nurturing,* and *cherishing.* First you take in all the goodness of the universe, including the wonderful fact that you are loved. Then you return that goodness, with your love, to the universe. First you take in your partner's special love for you with every inhalation. Then you return that love as you exhale. Both of you are enriched in the process. What better way than this could there be to demonstrate that both aspects of a loving relationship are as natural as breathing?

Here are the directions for this very useful exercise.

- Begin alone.

- Decide which words you want to use as you inhale. You may choose *silver,* as in the original exercise. Or you may want to go with *loved, nurtured, cherished,* or any other word that reminds you that you are loved.

- Decide which words you will use as you exhale: *gold, loving, nurturing, cherishing,* and so on. These words will help you feel love for your partner and the world.

- Take five to ten minutes a day to practice this breathing technique. Quietly inhale and exhale, repeating the words you have chosen. Don't worry if your mind drifts off. That happens to everyone. Just bring yourself back to these gentle words as you breathe in and out.

After doing this exercise for a few days you may want to begin using it when you are with others. You may find this exercise particularly useful at times when you are starting to feel anxious, annoyed, or upset.

You and your partner might next try doing this breathing exercise together. If you do, you might achieve a relaxed state of mutual lovingness with each other. However, don't go into this exercise with expectations. Let whatever happens be good enough.

# Take in love at your growing edge

Writers from the Gestalt school of therapy describe what they call a person's *growing edge.* They imagine that each person is a little like an expanding circular galaxy. Deep inside, at the center of the galaxy, is your *comfort zone.* This area is very familiar to you. It feels safe. This is where you keep all the habits of a lifetime. We have little anxiety within this zone because it is safe.

Way outside the comfort zone is the area of the *complete unknown.* You might say that this is like the astronomer's idea of "dark matter." There's something out there all right, something completely unknown and impossible to describe. The complete unknown fills people with vague feelings of dread: "I don't know what's out there, and I'm not sure I want to find out."

The most interesting part of a person's life is at the growing edge. Metaphorically, this area is at the edge of your personal comfort zone, in the narrow space between the safe and the unsafe, the familiar and the unfamiliar, the known and the unknown. People feel excited when they reach their growing edge because they sense that here is where they can expand their sense of being. The growing edge is a little scary because you are venturing into new territory. But it's not terrifying because it's been within sight for a while.

The Unknown

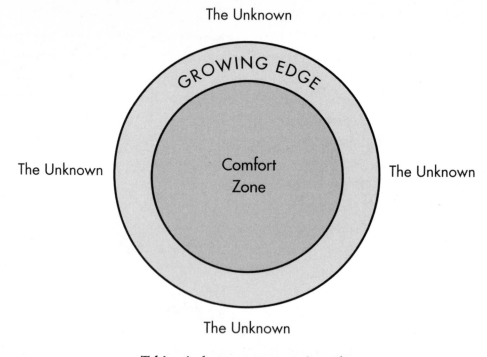

The Unknown                                                    The Unknown

The Unknown

**Taking in love at your growing edge**

Here's an example. Sheila grew up in a big city. However, she's always been drawn toward the outdoors. Once, several years ago, she considered just chucking her city life, buying a farm, and winging it. But she didn't follow through right then because she figured she'd fail at farming. And Sheila was right at that time. She didn't know enough to succeed. She signed up for some horticulture classes at the local university, took a master gardening class, and began raising cash crops on a small plot of land she rented from a nearby farmer. She became skillful. Then the farmer decided to retire. Sheila took a deep breath and bought his land. She still doesn't know if she will succeed, but she feels well enough prepared to take the chance. She's at her growing edge in life, the place between the known and the unknown.

You probably have growing edges in every major area of your life. Take work as an example. Certainly, there are aspects of your job you can almost do in your sleep. These are tasks within your comfort zone. Then there are other things you could never hope to do at all because they are in your unknown area. But finally there are duties you are just now beginning to tackle. You haven't mastered them yet so they take a lot of thought and energy. These new challenges exist at your growing edge. They may raise your anxiety a bit, but without these new challenges work would eventually become pretty boring.

Perhaps you've reached a growing edge in your religious or spiritual life. The old explanations of the meaning of life don't feel quite right anymore. Dissatisfied with what's inside your comfort zone, you may decide to try out a couple of new churches in your denomination. If that doesn't work, you may have to take another step, perhaps exploring another denomination or a more individualized spirituality. You're not planning to convert to an entirely new religion, though. That would be way past your growing edge and into the complete unknown.

We hope you have three particularly relevant growing edges right now. These are in the areas of saying "I love you," showing your partner your love, and taking in love. We'll focus on taking in love in this exercise. However, before we do that, please take a minute to answer these questions:

- How comfortable are you saying "I love you" to your partner?

- Are there any situations in which you cannot imagine telling him or her about your love? (For example, in public or during an argument. These are in your unknown area.)

- Where is your growing edge—where you are just learning to say "I love you" with your partner?

- Can you name a couple of ways you show love that are well within your comfort zone?

- Are there any ways your partner would like you to show him or her love that you cannot imagine doing, at least not yet? These are in your unknown area.

- How are you starting to show love in newer ways? (These new efforts on your part probably feel a little awkward and scary so far. However, you want to keep doing them until they become comfortable. These breakthrough areas are at your growing edge.)

Taking in love presents challenges for just about everybody. That means there are occasions and circumstances in which taking in your partner's love comes easily and naturally (when you are within your comfort zone), then there are probably times when you cannot imagine taking in love (maybe when your partner is angry with you or when you are very busy with something else). These situations exist in your unknown area. And then there are your growing edge opportunities—situations in which you are just learning how to take in your partner's love and caring.

Here are a few questions to help you discover your growing edge challenges about taking in love. Please take the time to write down your answers.

Can you think of situations in which your partner's attempts to show you love make you feel a little awkward, embarrassed, or uncomfortable?

_____

_____

_____

Why do you feel uncomfortable? What about you (not your partner) limits your ability to accept these particular ways of taking in love?

_____

_____

_____

Now imagine yourself becoming more comfortable taking in your partner's love in those situations. What would you be thinking, feeling, or doing differently?

_____

_____

_____

In general, with regard to taking in your partner's love, what is the single most important thing you need to tell yourself?

_____

_____

In general, with regard to taking in your partner's love, what behaviors do you most need to change? (These are actions that keep you from taking in love that you need to quit doing and/or things that would help you take in love that you need to start doing.)

I need to quit   _____

I need to start   _____

If you were to take the next twenty-four hours at your growing edge in terms of taking in your partner's love, what would you do?

_____

_____

When you take time at the growing edge, you eventually become more and more relaxed with what's out there. Those challenges get less scary and gradually become part of your now expanded comfort zone. So take a minute to close your eyes and imagine yourself being completely comfortable while accepting your partner's love in one of the situations you've been writing about. How would that feel?

_____

_____

_____

Will you let yourself move in that direction?

_____

_____

# Let love in even though you've been hurt before

Human beings have a natural reaction to pain: they want to avoid it as much as possible. That simple desire protects us from suffering needlessly and sometimes keeps us alive. Unfortunately, though, it's possible to get too good at avoiding potentially painful situations, especially in the area of taking in another's love.

Here's what happens.

You fall in love with someone

Who promises to always love, cherish, and respect you.

But instead hurts and even betrays you.

So you end that relationship emotionally damaged.

And then maybe it happens again.

And that's when you decide to stay distant.

"I'm no fool," you say to yourself. "Why should I open myself up to more heartache by loving and trusting someone new? Look what's happened to me already. I'm better off shutting down my need for others. True, I'm a little lonely now, but at least I'm safe. I'll never let anyone break my heart again." You stop trusting others, even the people who say they love you.

### Smart Idea

The question isn't whether I'll

Get hurt again. Of course I will.

We hurt each other unintended

When not trying. What I want to ask

Myself is whether this particular relationship

Will be worth whatever pain it may engender.

—INSPIRED BY ERICH FROMM

Although we're describing adult love relationships here, it is possible that you began shutting out others much earlier in life. Maybe in childhood you made a decision to stay safe by not letting people get close to you. That sometimes happens when parents are unreliable or dangerous, when someone you loved a lot died, or sometimes just because members of your family weren't very good at expressing love and so you quit hoping for it. Perhaps you've never recovered from when your first real love fell apart in your teens. Sure, others tell you to get over that lost love and get on with life, but it's not that easy. Whenever the disaster struck, whether you were ten years old, twenty, or forty, it had a devastating effect. It made you scared to fall in love again. Ever since then you've played life safer, like an investor hedging his or her bets to be sure not to lose rather than playing to win.

We want to suggest, strongly, that it's time to accept the pain from your past by letting it stay in the past. Yes, you've been hurt, badly hurt. But it's over. You survived. You've learned enough from whatever happened to protect yourself better. You've also probably learned one of life's most bittersweet truths: bad things can happen to you no matter how good and decent a person you are. We're not suggesting that you set yourself up for abuse or betrayal. No. You have every right to protect yourself. But isn't it time, *now*, for you to start letting in love from those people who have earned your trust? There's no sense waiting for some guarantee that you'll never be hurt again because life never offers such certainties.

Are you ready to let more love in by letting go of the past? If so, answer these questions.

Do you remember a specific time in your life when someone you love or loved broke your heart? _____

If so, what happened?

_____

_____

_____

How has that episode in your life most limited your ability to take in love?

_____

_____

_____

How fair is it to say that your main goal in the area of love has been to stay safe—not to get hurt again—rather than to take the chance of letting in love?

_____

_____

_____

How fair is it to say that you avoid taking in love because you are afraid to deeply trust anybody, even your partner?

_____

_____

_____

What thoughts do you have (such as "I can't trust anybody" or "I've been too hurt to ever really fall in love again") that keep you from fully opening yourself to your partner's love?

_____

_____

_____

What thoughts could you have that would help you let yourself take in love? Here are some possibilities and space to add your own.

_____ Today I choose to trust my partner.

_____ It's time for me to let go of the past.

_____ The person in my life today is named _____, not

_____.

_____ I won't let myself be limited by my past any longer.

_____ I'm ready to quit playing life so safe.

_____ Today I'll let myself feel my partner's love.

_____  _____.

_____  _____.

# Take in love and comfort even when you have difficulty loving yourself

Therapists talk about how good parents create a "holding environment" around their children. That means the parents are there when their children are hurt, sad, or overwhelmed. Well, we grown-ups can do the same thing for our partners. Your partner in life can help you feel safe, warm, and, most important, loved when you are stressed out, hurting, angry, or sad, or when you have lost confidence in yourself—but only if you let him or her do that for you. Maybe at those times you feel totally unlovable, but that doesn't mean your partner has to agree. He or she knows you are worth loving. After all, your partner has chosen to be your partner for some good reasons.

You've probably heard these sayings: "You can't give love to others if you don't love yourself" and "You can only take in another's love to the extent you love yourself." There must be some truth to them, or people wouldn't repeat them as often as they do. Certainly the young woman who responds to her lover's "I love you" with "Oh, how could you? I'm not worth loving" is taking in love only to the extent that she loves herself. Her lover's words create what's called cognitive dissonance between what she believes about herself ("I am unlovable") and what she hears ("You are loved").

SMART PRINCIPLE

If you are having trouble

Loving yourself real well,

Then just borrow some from me,

For I love you infinitely.

195

Some people do believe they are basically unlovable. They may go so far as to believe they are God's mistake—a total failure of being. If you are like that, you will need to do some personal work so you can take in the love of the people around you. See our book *Letting Go of Shame* to connect the feeling of being unlovable with the concept of shame.

However, it would be a big mistake for you, or for anybody using this book, to wait until you are "healthy" and completely self-loving before taking in another's love. That's because taking in another's love creates feelings of self-love and self-worth inside you.

Here's a typical example. One evening Mary is feeling particularly bad about herself. She seems to have screwed up everything she's tried today: she did badly on a test at school, she made a serious mistake at work, her kids told her she was mean because she wouldn't let them out of their chores, and finally, just to make her day even worse, she broke one of her favorite coffee cups, spilling hot coffee all over her blouse in the process.

Now in walks her partner, Charlie. "Hi," he says. "How are you doing?" Mary dissolves into tears. "Terrible," she replies and tells him about her day. "Well," Charlie responds, "I'm sad for you that all that happened. But you know I love you. Can I give you a hug?" So now what are Mary's options?

1. She could push him away with a "Don't even bother, I'm not worth loving" statement. Result: They'll both feel isolated, and Mary's self-esteem will probably drop through the floor.

2. She could let him hug her but keep telling herself she's such a loser that he's a fool to love her. That way it looks like she's taking in Charlie's love, but she's really not. Result: Charlie might believe things are better for a while, but Mary's self-worth will only get lower. She'll also be building deception into the relationship.

3. She could graciously accept the love that is offered by letting Charlie hug her while thinking something like, "Okay. No matter how bad a day I had, Charlie still loves me. Maybe I'm not such a horrible person after all." Result: Mary not only feels a little better about

herself, she actually feels both loved and lovable. She lets Charlie be her "holding environment" for a little while, just like a child receiving comfort from a parent.

Here's an exercise designed to help you do two things: (1) discover the thoughts you have that make it hard for you to receive your partner's love when you are unhappy with yourself and (2) help you change those thoughts to ones that will help you take in his or her comforting love.

Below are several thoughts people have that go with feeling unlovable. Beside each statement, place a number from 0 to 5, with 0 meaning "I never have that thought" and 5 meaning "I always think that way about myself when I get down on myself."

\_\_\_\_ I'm such a loser, nobody could love me.

\_\_\_\_ I'm so physically unattractive [ugly, fat, old] my partner doesn't like me anymore.

\_\_\_\_ I'm too dumb [stupid, idiotic] for my partner to be interested in anything I say.

\_\_\_\_ My partner would be better off without me.

\_\_\_\_ If I were my partner I wouldn't want to have anything to do with me.

\_\_\_\_ I'm too emotionally unstable for my partner to love me.

\_\_\_\_ I've been so bad in my life I don't deserve to be loved.

\_\_\_\_ I can't do anything right, so who could possibly love me? No one, that's who.

\_\_\_\_ I know I'm unlovable and I won't let anyone tell me otherwise, not even my partner.

\_\_\_\_ [Fill in your own statement here] _____

_____

Your job now is to challenge the thoughts above that you have given the highest scores. Here's how.

First, say to yourself, "That's B.S.! That statement isn't true. I've known it's not true for a long time. I won't keep thinking that negative thought when all it does is keep me from taking in my partner's love and caring when I most need it." *This is no time to be wishy-washy. You must be firm.* You must forcefully shove that old negative thought aside. That thought is not your friend.

Second, substitute a new thought that feels acceptable to you. Again, don't be wishy-washy. For instance, it won't do much good to say, "Well, maybe I look good enough that my partner doesn't find me totally disgusting." Come on! You need to say something like this: "I know I am attractive to my partner. He [She] tells me so every day. I'm going to let myself believe it right now."

This third step is optional but highly recommended. Tell your partner about the old thought and the new one so you can get some immediate reward and reassurance, like, "Honey, that's wonderful. Of course I find you attractive. I've been hoping you'd believe me."

Here's space for you to work.

First thought to challenge: _____
_____

New thought: _____
_____

Second thought to challenge: _____
_____

New thought: _____
_____

Third thought to challenge: _____

_____

New thought: _____

_____


Now start telling those old thoughts to get lost, practicing those new thoughts, and seeking affirmation from your partner.

# Act "as if" you believe people love you until you actually believe it

The idea of acting "as if" comes from Alcoholics Anonymous, where reluctant newcomers to the program were told to act as if they really wanted to stay sober. People who act that way go to AA meetings, stay out of bars, read the Big Book, find a sponsor, and so on. The idea is that someone doing these activities will gradually begin to like being sober. Then they'll go from acting "as if" to really being in recovery.

Perhaps you have trouble taking in your partner's love. If so, then acting "as if" is a good way to start doing so.

Here's an example of someone who needs to act "as if." Recently we were having a couples counseling session with a woman we'll call Judy. Judy had suffered many terrible losses and betrayals when she was young. She had been abused and abandoned. Her parents had beaten her. Worst of all, Judy had been told again and again that nobody would ever love her. She absorbed these messages and grew into an adult who believed she was fundamentally unlovable. She then entered into a series of bad relationships with mean, angry men. None of these men helped her feel better about herself. They all contributed to Judy's belief that she was not worthy of love. By age forty Judy found herself depressed, fearful, and lonely.

Then Paul came along. Paul was shy, a man who had never had a serious relationship with a woman. He could be crude. He could be thoughtless. He wasn't God's gift to women. But he was a good man who was capable of really loving a woman.

Paul and Judy began dating. They made a commitment. They fell in love. They married. That could have been the end of the story. But there was one problem that brought them to counseling. Paul explained that he simply never felt that Judy really took in his love. Every time he said, "Judy, I love you" or anything like that she'd say something like, "Yeah, sure you do" or " Uh-huh; that's nice." Or she'd completely ignore him. Or maybe she'd say, "I love you, too, Paul" in a mechanical way that didn't feel quite right. Paul added that he was certain Judy loved him. That wasn't his concern. He just wished she could fully accept his love.

We asked Paul to tell Judy he loved her. He did so and even explained how much he appreciated her caring, how physically attractive he found her, how much he enjoyed her sense of humor. Judy heard his words. She looked as if she was trying to take them in. But all the time her head was moving horizontally, just a little, a subtle way for her to tell us that she couldn't believe it. "No, no," she said nonverbally. "I'm not lovable, so you can't love me." Also, she wouldn't look directly at Paul while he was talking. Avoiding eye contact, of course, is an excellent way for Judy to keep from feeling connected to Paul.

What can Judy do so she can accept Paul's love? That's where acting "as if" comes in. Judy has to change her behavior to reflect the ways people who believe they are lovable act. That means no head shaking or avoiding eye contact. Instead, she needs to keep still while looking at him. That way Judy gives herself a chance to learn how to take in Paul's love.

So what about you? How much are you like Judy? Like her, do you need to act "as if" in order to learn how to accept being loved?

Here is an exercise that will help you act "as if."

First, give yourself some time to observe how others take in love. If your partner is good at it, casually tell him or her "I love you" and notice how he or she takes it in. Watch other people as well—anyone who seems comfortable receiving love, appreciation, and affection. Take at least

SMART SAYING

*Play the part and you shall become.*
—ANONYMOUS

twenty-four to forty-eight hours just to gather information. Write down what you observe here.

People who take in love _____

_____

_____

_____

Meanwhile, write down all the ways you deflect love. Here are several possibilities, but you may very well have others.

\_\_\_    I stay too busy to give anyone time to tell me I am loved.

\_\_\_    I don't listen when someone says I am loved.

\_\_\_    I tell others I love them first and try to keep attention on them.

\_\_\_    I don't make eye contact when someone says I am loved.

\_\_\_    I shake my head.

\_\_\_    I don't do anything obvious, but I tell myself I am unlovable.

\_\_\_    I don't breathe when someone says I am loved.

\_\_\_    I argue with people who say I am loved. I try to talk them out of it.

\_\_\_    I consciously avoid situations in which people might tell me I am loved.

\_\_\_    I do unloving things to keep people from loving me too much.

\_\_\_    Other (What?) _____

\_\_\_    Other (What?) _____

Now write down the three most important things—actual behaviors, not changes in attitude or beliefs—that you need to do in order to better take in your partner's love. This will be your personal "as if" list.

1. _____

2. _____

3. _____

You are trying to develop a new habit here. So you must give yourself plenty of time. Take the next week or two to practice changing your actions. If you're comfortable, ask your partner for help. Have him or her say "I love you" so you can try out your new behavior. You should get the hang of it soon. Then taking in love will feel more natural and you'll go from acting "as if" to really feeling loved.

# The hole in the bucket problem: Recognize and understand why you have trouble taking in love

Sally and Larry have just made love. Good love. Caring love. That's when Sally turns to Larry and murmurs, "I love you with all my heart." So what does Larry say? "Yeah, honey, that's really nice. I love you, too." But what does he think? "I wish I could believe that. I wish I could let myself feel loved. But I just can't seem to take in love."

Larry's not the only person in the universe who has difficulty taking in love. In fact, he's got plenty of company, perhaps including you. Larry suffers from what we call the "hole in the bucket" problem. Here's what that's like.

Imagine how simple life would be if each of us carried around a container labeled PLEASE PUT ALL YOUR LOVE FOR ME IN THIS BUCKET. We could go around from person to person asking for love and they would know exactly where and how to give us that love. "Just put it in the bucket," we could say, and then we could hold that love right where we could see it all the time.

But what if your bucket had a big hole in it? Sure, you could go up to people and ask for love. They might be happy to give you some, too. But what would happen? The love would fall right through the bucket! When you peeked into that bucket it would be empty. You'd certainly feel disappointed. You'd probably feel unloved. You might even feel unlovable. Perhaps you would start believing that nobody really cared about you. Finally, you might just give up, deciding that you will never be loved.

Notice, though, that the problem here is not with others. The hole in the bucket is the problem. Others do love you. They keep putting love into the bucket. But the bucket doesn't hold that love long enough for you to feel it. Furthermore, it's your bucket, nobody else's. So the big question here is, how can you mend your bucket so you can actually hold the love that people offer?

Before we go on to that question, though, check off the sentence or sentences that best describe the bucket you carry around to take in love.

Unnecessary pain. That's what people feel when they can't take in the love others offer. Useless pain. But why suffer when you don't have to? Start mending your bucket today so you can quit feeling lonely when you could feel loved.

_____ My bucket is solid and whole. I'm good at taking in love.

_____ My bucket has a few tiny cracks in it. My feeling of being loved leaks away slowly.

_____ My bucket has a small hole in it. That means I can take in large acts of love, but sometimes I don't notice little acts of caring.

_____ My bucket has a huge hole in it. It's really hard for me to keep feeling loved even when my partner or others are very loving toward me.

_____ Bucket? What bucket? I quit carrying that around a long time ago.

By the way, how do you imagine people responding to you as you go around asking for contributions to your love bucket? Do you see them smiling and gladly throwing in love? Maybe you see them holding back, only slowly and reluctantly making an offering. Or possibly you visualize them turning you down: "No thanks, we already gave today." Worse yet, what if they were to turn and walk away with a "Don't bother me with that—I'm too busy" attitude? Remember, what you expect often predicts what you'll get. So it helps to anticipate that others will gladly want to fill your bucket when you ask them. And why shouldn't they? There's plenty of love to go around. Filling your bucket won't empty theirs.

Let's head back to the main question: *how can you mend your bucket so you get better at taking in and holding your partner's love?*

## Step One: Take Responsibility Now, in the Present, for Carrying Around a Damaged Bucket

It certainly would be interesting to understand how your bucket became damaged. That's the stuff of therapy, journaling, and hard work. But right now it doesn't really matter how that bucket got broken. That's because whatever happened cannot be undone. There simply is no magic answer in the past that will fix your love bucket. So the first step you need to take is to accept sole responsibility for the state of your bucket.

## Step Two: Gather the Equipment You'll Need to Fix Your Bucket

You'll need the emotional equivalents of a soldering iron, solder, and new metal. Select the action tools you'll need from the following list.

_____ Making a commitment to take in my partner's love without doubting or questioning

_____ Gaining the courage to directly ask for my partner's love

_____ Learning the mechanics of taking in love (see Exercise 37, "Give your partner opportunities to be loving")

_____ Letting go of the past so I can take in the love offered now

_____ Listening better so I can actually hear when others tell me they love me

_____ Feeling confident that I am worth loving

_____ Reminding myself every day that I really am deeply loved

_____ Accepting more physical touch and holding without stiffening up

_____ Visualizing myself having a mended and overflowing love bucket

_____ Allowing myself to notice when I feel connected with my partner

_____ Something else (What? _____)

## Step Three: Fix the Bucket

This step is the easiest of the three if you have prepared well. You've gathered your tools, which means you are fully prepared to mend the bucket. Now you need to take action. That means utilizing all those tools today, tomorrow, and the next day. One way to do so is to select one tool a day that you will concentrate on. Start with the single most important tool from the list you just made. If it's visualizing a mended and overflowing love bucket, then today, several times, take a few minutes to visualize exactly that. If it's making a commitment to take in your partner's love without doubting or questioning, do that, strongly and consciously. Then select another tool to use the next day. By selecting a new tool each day, you will get better at using them all.

Which tool do you need to begin with in order to mend your love bucket?

_____

_____

Which tool comes next?

_____

_____

After that?

_____

_____

# Don't be greedy: Nobody owes you constant love or attention

Love is a wonderful gift, something to feel tremendously grateful to receive. As you are learning to take in love better, you are probably feeling more connected to your partner, more self-confident, and even a little more lovable. However, we want to warn you about one danger as you go about this process. The danger is that you might get greedy, wanting and demanding more and more of your partner's time and energy. If you forget to stay grateful, you might start believing that your partner is obligated to love you. You must remember that your partner owes you nothing, not even a single "I love you."

Have you ever heard of the phrase "entitlement fantasies"? Entitlement fantasies happen when people believe that they have a natural right to something so they don't have to work at getting it. Here are a few examples of people with entitlement fantasies.

> **SMART SAYING**
>
> *If your desires be endless, your cares and fears will be too.*
> —THOMAS FULLER

A teenager who thinks the world owes him or her an allowance, three meals a day, and a nice bed to sleep in—forever.

A spoiled child who refuses to share toys or food.

An adult with a "sob story" designed to make others take care of him or her.

Relationship partners sometimes have their own share of entitlement fantasies.

My partner should spend every minute with me.

My partner should know I love him [her] without my saying or doing anything.

My partner should heal all my wounds and make me feel whole.

My partner's only job in life is to make me feel good.

My partner should always be available when I need him [her].

My partner should always want what I want.

Greed is a central theme in all entitlement fantasies. It's as if one partner were a baby bird, screaming, "FEED ME, FEED ME, FEED ME!" to his or her partner. Somehow, no matter how much the partner tries, that baby bird stays hungry. "MORE! I WANT MORE!" demands the baby bird. Never completely satisfied, the baby bird complains that his or her partner isn't loving enough, caring enough, thoughtful enough. Whatever that person's partner does then feels like too little, too late. Meanwhile, sooner or later, that person's partner may get tired of this endless task and may even start asking, "Hey, wait a minute here. What about me? Don't I ever get fed?"

Now, everybody has at least a little of that baby bird inside him or her. Who doesn't harbor a wish that the universe would take care of his or her every want and need? And perhaps you've been hungry for love for a long time. Maybe you felt more like you were starving for love than just hungering for it. Now that you're starting to feel loved you can't get enough. It's not that you want to be greedy, demanding, or ungrateful. It's just that you've been hungry for so long that you don't want to quit eating just yet. You have a tremendous need for reassurance that your partner does truly love you.

Is all this sounding familiar to you in your relationship? If you are too hungry for love you've probably heard your partner say things like:

You're never satisfied no matter what I do to show you my love.

I tell you I love you, but you can't seem to take it in.

I try to give you what you want, but it's never enough.

Sometimes I feel like you're trying to make me part of you.

You never believe me when I say I love you.

I wish you would accept the love I have for you.

The more I give the more you want.

Can't you just relax about us once in a while?

I'm not your mother [father], and I can't make up for what they didn't give you.

I love you. I love you. I love you. How many times do you need me to say it?

You are so insecure. I'm not going to leave you.

On the other hand, maybe it's you who has been making those statements. If so, you need to talk with your partner. Tell that person you are concerned because he or she seems unable to take in your love.

How can you break free from this kind of excessive need for love and reassurance? Well, if we were talking about a problem with overeating someone might suggest that you chew your food a little more slowly. That way you can taste food better and your stomach has time to send a signal when it's full. Perhaps that same idea would help here. Could you make a commitment to yourself to take in the love that your partner offers a little more slowly and thoughtfully? If so, select a few sentences from the following list. These thoughts will help you let go of your hunger if you think about them regularly. They will let you more truly enjoy the love you're getting:

\_\_\_\_ I do feel loved right now.

\_\_\_\_ I'm not starving for love so I don't have to beg for more.

\_\_\_\_ I am a lovable human being.

\_\_\_\_ I am a loved human being.

_____ I don't need to be greedy or demanding about getting love from my partner.

_____ My glass is half full.

_____ I can choose right now to be satisfied with the love my partner gives me.

_____ I accept the love my partner gives me.

_____ My partner can't always be there for me and that's okay.

_____ I won't let old fears or wounds keep me from enjoying my partner's love.

_____ I won't ask for more than my partner can give me.

_____ I can't enjoy a good meal if I won't let myself taste it.

_____ My partner's love for me is good enough. It doesn't have to be perfect.

We suggest that you write down three or four of these sentences (or any others you have come up with that would be helpful) on a sheet of paper that you can carry with you in your wallet or purse. That way you can look at them whenever you need to remind yourself not to be greedy about love.

# My lover's love is like . . . Writing analogies and a story about your partner's love

My love is like a red, red rose. You've certainly heard that line before. Phrases like this are called analogies. They are very powerful because they help us view things in totally new ways. They also seem to connect the left and right parts of our brains, linking the known with the unknown, the literal with the imaginary.

People spend hours trying to describe their love for their partners. My love is like a rose, an apple, a lightning bolt, a Maserati, a snowmobile, an endless dream, a picture frame waiting for your portrait. . . . Some of these analogies are easy to understand because they touch something universal ("My love is like a rose" connects two beautiful objects, your lover and the most magnificent of all flowers) while others might be totally unique (if someone said, "My love is like a geometry quiz," you would probably have to ask him or her to explain how in the world a geometry quiz is like love).

So how would you describe your love for your partner?

My love is like a _____.

Love analogies like this don't have to be about your love for your partner. Let's turn this game around and ask you to think about how you feel when you fully take in your partner's love. Here are some possibilities.

> **SMART SAYING**
>
> *Every bird flies with its own wings.*
> —SWAHILI PROVERB

Taking in my partner's love is like . . .

Closing my eyes and feeling a soft breeze caressing my face

Being held in God's hands

Smelling cinnamon rolls baking in the oven

Getting the giggles and not wanting to stop

Winning a billion dollars in the lottery

Reading a great book

Being the star pitcher on a first-place team

Relaxing in a warm bath while all my troubles fade away

Listening as often as I want to my favorite song

Being a puppy snuggling in for a nap in the middle of the litter

Skydiving just after I open the parachute

Going to a surprise party only to discover that the party is for me

_____

_____

We left a couple of lines for you to write your own analogies.

Now, analogies are wonderful one-line descriptions of what it feels like to take in your partner's love. They are like short stories. But perhaps you are ready to write a book instead of a short story. In that case, you'll need at least two things to get started: a title and an outline of the chapters. Here's a sample.

Book title: *I Was Too Busy for Love—But Not Anymore*

Chapter One: Why I Decided I'd Never Let Anyone Love Me

Chapter Two: How I Kept Myself Too Busy for Love

Chapter Three: I Thought I Was Happy—but I Was Empty Inside

Chapter Four: And Then She Entered My Life

Chapter Five: I Tried to Keep Her out of My Heart

Chapter Six: The Day I Decided to Let In Her Love

Chapter Seven: She Loves Me. Now I Know It. Now I Believe It. Now I Feel It. I Am Blessed

What's the title for your book about learning how to take in your partner's love?

_____

And what are the titles for your chapters?

Chapter 1: _____

Chapter 2: _____

Chapter 3: _____

Chapter 4: _____

Chapter 5: _____

Chapter 6: _____

Chapter 7: _____

Do you think your book will have a happy ending? Why shouldn't it? You're the author.

# The spiritual aspects of taking in your partner's love

The word *spirituality* comes from a Latin term meaning "to breathe." Spirituality, then, implies a special way of inhaling. We feel spiritual when we breathe in the universe and allow ourselves to feel deeply connected with everything around us. That is when we feel most connected to God, ourselves, and others. Breathing in the universe fills us with wonder, awe, joy, and love. We sense during these moments that there is God in every-one and everything. And, especially, we sense that there is a piece of God within our partner. We realize that our partner is special, wonderful, unique, and infinite. We celebrate that person's existence then and become warmly appreciative that he or she is in our life. This celebration of our partner makes spiritual intimacy possible.

True intimacy is spiritual. That's because intimacy involves two people giving and receiving each other's most private, vulnerable aspects: their secrets, yearnings, hopes, and dreams. This kind of sharing transforms the self. A person is never quite the same after having shared that deeply of oneself with one's partner. He or she senses a tremendous connection, a feeling of communion. Belonging takes on new meaning at this spiritual level. You are no longer walking down the path of life alone. Nor are you simply walking down the path of life beside your partner. Instead, you have taken your partner into your heart. You are walking down that path together, holding hands, forever. Belonging like this is a healing experience. By feeling deeply loved by our partner we feel less shame and more love for ourselves. Accepting our partner without judgment helps us judge ourselves less as well. We become part of a whole, creating an "us" that brings a feeling of completion, connection, and commitment. Spiritually united, we feel the infinite in the intimate and the intimate in the infinite.

Taking in your partner's love at the spiritual level is always possible but never easy. You must suspend judgment, criticism, and doubt in favor of acceptance, celebration, and understanding. The most important thing to remember is that you are very, very fortunate to have this person in your life.

Here are a few questions that will help you take in your partner's love at the spiritual level.

What about your partner fills you with wonder, awe, and fascination?

_____

_____

_____

When have you felt truly grateful and humble to receive your partner's love?

_____

_____

_____

Do you believe that there is a part of God in your partner? If so, when do you most see, hear, feel, or sense that aspect of him or her?

_____

_____

_____

Can you think of a time when you have felt spiritually united with your partner? If so, write down your memories of that experience.

_____

_____

_____

How has (or could) taking in your partner's love transformed you? Made you into a different or better person?

_____

_____

_____

How has (or could) taking in your partner's love deepened your sense of spirituality? Of belonging in this universe? Of connection and communion?

_____

_____

_____

Right now, at this moment, how can you let yourself take in your partner's love as a spiritual gift?

_____

_____

_____

# References

Bartholomew, Kim, Antonia Henderson, and Donald Dutton (2001). "Insecure Attachment and Abusive Intimate Relationships." In Clulow, Christopher (ed.), *Adult Attachment and Couple Psychotherapy.* London: Brunner-Routledge.

Berecz, John (2001). "All That Glitters Is Not Gold: Bad Forgiving in Counseling and Preaching." *Pastoral Psychology* 49(4): 253–275.

Bowlby, John (1969). *Attachment.* New York: Basic Books.

Ciaramicoli, Arthur (2000). *The Power of Empathy.* New York: Dutton.

Gottman, John M., and Nan Silver (2000). *The Seven Principles for Making Marriage Work.* New York: Three Rivers Press.

Hargrave, Terry (1997). *Families and Forgiveness: Healing Wounds in the Intergenerational Family.* New York: Taylor & Francis.

Kaufman, Gershen (1996). *The Psychology of Shame*, 2nd ed. New York: Springer.

Potter-Efron, Patricia, and Ronald Potter-Efron (1999). *The Secret Message of Shame.* Oakland, Calif.: New Harbinger Publications.

Potter-Efron, Ronald (1998). *Being, Belonging, Doing.* Oakland, Calif.: New Harbinger Publications.

Potter-Efron, Ronald, and Patricia Potter-Efron (1989). *Letting Go of Shame.* Center City, Minn.: Hazelden Publications.

# Index